CHILD TRAFFICKING
The Fight for Freedom

SURESH KUMAR

INDIA · SINGAPORE · MALAYSIA

Copyright © Suresh Kumar 2022
All Rights Reserved.

ISBN 978-1-68586-732-4

This book has been published with all efforts taken to make the material error-free after the consent of the author. However, the author and the publisher do not assume and hereby disclaim any liability to any party for any loss, damage, or disruption caused by errors or omissions, whether such errors or omissions result from negligence, accident, or any other cause.

While every effort has been made to avoid any mistake or omission, this publication is being sold on the condition and understanding that neither the author nor the publishers or printers would be liable in any manner to any person by reason of any mistake or omission in this publication or for any action taken or omitted to be taken or advice rendered or accepted on the basis of this work. For any defect in printing or binding the publishers will be liable only to replace the defective copy by another copy of this work then available.

Dedication

Dedicated to Professor L. Pushpa Kumar, Faculty of Law, University of Delhi, who constantly encouraged me to write a book on child trafficking; all the child trafficking survivors who have been trying to free the world of all forms of trafficking; my parents whose blessings kept me going through thick and thin; and to my daughter Medhavi Sharma and wife Rinku Sharma who sacrificed family-bonding time and outings for me to write this book.

To Chelsee,

To make our meeting a memorable one.

With best Compliments

[signature]
28.06.2022

Written after years of immersive research as an anti-trafficking footsoldier, this book fills an important gap in our understanding of why child labour persists in India. Suresh Kumar draws from personal experience in scores of child rescue operations and from evolving policy measures to present rich insights into how trafficking works, the compulsions in impoverished regions and the impact on young minds. Most startling are the narratives of the survivors, raw and resilient.

– *Kavitha Iyer*, Journalist and Writer

Contents

Acknowledgement 9

1. Trafficking of Children 13
2. Prosecution of the Child Traffickers 53
3. Dream of Clearing the Secondary Exam Comes True 67
4. Succumbing to Long Working Hours, Hunger and Lack of Medical Care 74
5. Familial Trafficking 89
6. Can Prosecution Prevent Child Trafficking? 97
7. Most of the Child Labourers Are Musahars 111
8. Efficiency of Anti-Human Trafficking Units in the Country 117

9. Survivors Hardly Get Their Compensations 123

10. Silver Lining For Survivors: Draft of
    Anti-Trafficking Bill-2021 127

Appendix.. 133

Acknowledgement

A big thanks to Centre DIRECT for providing me an opportunity to work with its anti-child trafficking projects, enabling me to connect with the child trafficking survivors and their families.

Thanks to Ashish, Rahul, Rakesh, Shibu and Radhe Kumar for trusting me with their stories. I'm grateful that they made time for in-person interviews, and that they also accommodated several follow-up phone calls.

I would like to thank Deenanath Maurya, Vijay Kevat, Ranjan Yadav, Umesh Ram, Raj Thakur, Venkatesh Sharma, Archana Kumari, Varun Kumar, Sagorika Laha, Rakhi Singh, Vimal Kumar Mantu, Ram Ratan Singh, Madhuri Krishna and Sarvesh Manjhi for explaining the intricacies of the child trafficking networks in Bihar. I'm thankful to Ashish for patiently answering all my weirdly specific questions about every tiny little detail.

I would like to thank Sanjog, a Kolkata-based organisation that has been fighting against human trafficking for over a decade. The organisation which was also the recipient of the Stop Slavery Impact Award-2021 has commissioned outstanding studies along with their anti-trafficking activities and has allowed me to quote their research findings.

* * *

Disclaimer: This book is based largely on the inputs provided by child trafficking survivors with lived experiences, their families, social workers, lawyers, researchers and experts combating child trafficking.

Note: The real names of child trafficking survivors have been used only in instances when they are adults and explicit consent has been provided to do so. In all other instances, names have been changed to protect the privacy of the survivors.

1
Trafficking of Children

It was nearly dusk when money changed hands. Sikander, a henchman for a local child trafficker paid an advance of the two thousand rupees to Sheela Devi, a daily wager and Ashish's mother. It was the last week of June 2015. Sikander had struck similar deals with the six other parents from the same village; a total of seven children in the age group of 9-13 years. It was a windfall for Sikander. All the children belonged to the same caste: Musahar.

Before the trafficking, a lot of instructions were given to the children. The children were asked to say that they were going to Jaipur to see their parents, who work in factories there. However, Sikander was vague about their destination, lest the children be questioned by the police, representatives of childline, or charity organisations. The kids just had to nod their heads with their dull eyes and poker faces. "If someone asks who is accompanying you, tell them that your uncle is," Sikander told the children while puffing a cigarette.

When Ashish's mother told him to get ready for a place, a place she hadn't heard of before and had become a tongue twister for her, he did not know where the deal—which promised a regular income for his family and education for him—would take him. "What work will I have to do?" he asked his mother. She replied in a clouded tone that the work would be in a bangle-making factory; quite easy to adapt to, work only for four hours a day, the rest of the day to be spent in a private convent school studying his favourite subjects. Sikander had promised them four thousand rupees per month. The family dreamed of upgrading to a pukka house; sleeping well even during rainy days when they wouldn't have to wake up to a flooded house. Ashish looked askance at his mother.

His mother had never been to school, nor had his father. The 13-year-old who was in sixth standard was a precocious student with dreams of becoming a teacher when he grew up. He would go door-to-door in his community, and counsel parents to send their children to school regularly. With his efforts, school attendance, in general, was quite high in the village school. Ashish sensed something amiss and requested his mother to change her mind. He assured her that he would work locally and supplement the family's income, but to no avail. His parents were landless, daily-wage agricultural labourers. His mother wanted to give him a good life, and for her, this was like a dream coming true. She also wanted him to become an educated man, although she was not sure about the trafficker providing Ashish education. He could not sleep the whole night, rolling over a polythene sheet and staring at the roof of his tiny mud hut with barely enough room to stand up. The next morning, he was given a packet containing a few rotis, some mango pickle and water in a Coca-Cola bottle, which he had caught hold of during a marriage ceremony in his village. The function held by an upper-caste family, that was relatively better off, had served cold drinks. Ashish had picked up two good-shaped bottles from a pile of garbage the following morning. He used one of those bottles to fill water and keep beside him at night to quench his thirst whenever he woke up. The other bottle was reserved to be filled with water to be used by his father when he stepped out for open defection, as they didn't have a toilet at home.

Ashish did not want to go to the place that his mother wanted him to. He had doubts about the offer. He again requested his mother to change her mind and return the advance of two thousand rupees that she had received from

Sikander. But she did not change her mind, and Ashish had to accept the decision of his mother grumpily. He decided to trust his fate despite serious doubts shrouding the offer for a promised good life.

The following day, the children were ready to set out for their destinations in their best clothes, and three of them were in their school uniforms. School uniforms are given to government school students by the Bihar government. All seven children were divided into groups. To escape the prying eyes in the village, they were instructed to walk around five kilometres to a nearby village to catch a waiting auto, which would then drop them off at the Gaya railway station. The children arrived at the railway station. It was their first time at the railway station. All the children were exhausted, summer temperatures in Gaya were soaring. They spent all the day at the railway station to catch a night train—Jharkhand SJ Express. The train is widely used by migrant labourers of Jharkhand to get to Delhi and is locally known as the Hatia-Anand Vihar Express.

At the railway station, one more child, 12-year-old Rahul joined them. He was from a different administrative block of the same district. Now, they became a group of eight children destined to endure bondage in the bangle factory.

Meanwhile, locks of their hair were dyed blonde, so that they could be easily identified and easily huddled all the way to bangle factories in Jaipur, Rajasthan—the bangle-making hub of the country. Each one of them was given a general ticket to New Delhi and made to sit in groups of two in four different compartments within the same coach. They were monitored by someone sitting far away in the same coach, he kept moving places while maintaining distance, to avoid falling into trouble. Many charity organisations working towards combating child labour and child trafficking de-board children and get the traffickers arrested by the police. Quite a good number of childlines and charity organisations work on high alert in sensitive railway stations where incidences of child exploitation and child trafficking are reportedly high. The rescued children are sent back to their families without harm. The police also keep a watch out for the movement of children in clusters and do approach such children if their presence may raise suspicions.

However, no such attempts were made by either the police or any charity organisation during their 1085 km journey to New Delhi. Albeit a police constable who was part of the train escorting team did ask Rakesh to show his ticket. When asked about his destination, Rakesh replied promptly, "I am going to Jaipur. My father works there." Ashish sitting next to him was a bit nervous and started drinking water, he continued drinking water till the police constable moved ahead murmuring something which Ashish could not make out. Many food vendors passed through the compartment, even though the children were hungry they could not buy anything as they did not have a single penny with them.

Sikander who met them in the village while briefing them about the nature of the job and precautions to be exercised during the journey was not seen once the children set out on their journey. However, they were given food and water during the travel up to Delhi by somebody else who did not share his name although once he was asked for it by one of the children.

The children were worried if he would ask them for money; a young migrant worker in their village, who just returned from Mumbai, had told them that a lot of cheating of various kinds happened in trains. Be very alert during the journey! The train was full of passengers, giving the impression that there was only one train that ferried weekly from Jharkhand to Delhi via Gaya in Bihar. The children could not sleep, even though they were drowsy. It was a tiring sleepless night for them.

They arrived in Delhi the next day. They were received by another stranger who took them to a bus stand to catch the Jaipur-bound bus. He spoke Hindi with a Rajasthani tone making it difficult for the children to understand him. Every time he spoke, children looked at his face in utter confusion. Hours later they reached the bangle factory in a neighbourhood called Kho Nagoriyan. It was a small room on the first floor of a multi-storeyed building with an attached bathroom. There was no ceiling fan. These eight children were grudgingly received by four other children. All emotionless children, completely robbed of their childhood, who had been working for months. This experience was a shock for the newly arrived children. They crammed into the space and crashed for hours after the long and uncomfortable journey.

A Terrible Beginning

The next morning, Ashish and the other children were taken to a different building in the same location. They were put in a tiny, dilapidated room with eleven more children under a trainer-cum-supervisor who had come to the factory when he was 12 years old, from Gaya, and had been promoted to the rank of supervisor. They started living cheek by jowl—nineteen people in the stuffy one-window room without a fan, where seepage and cobwebs covered the walls.

They were given two rotis and some pieces of fried potato as breakfast, and a limited amount of water. They were completely unaware that they had landed in a desert state where water was scant. Soon, it became a new normal for them: taking bath once a week and drinking a limited amount of water. There was a water jar kept in the room, one jar per day to be shared by them all, whenever the water was consumed completely, they had to stay thirsty till the next day.

And, there were instructions to be strictly followed:

1. No one should step out.
2. No talking.
3. No requests for making phone calls to parents or anyone else.
4. No rest during the day.
5. Food shall be served strictly at the given times.
6. No demand for extra food.
7. Eat less and work more.
8. Sleep late and wake up early.
9. No crying out for families.
10. No complaints about fever or headache.
11. Come what may, no holidays.

12. And, those who don't abide by the rules are subject to severe beating with a strong baton that is kept in the corner of the room.

In the beginning, at least one of them had to undergo severe beatings every day. This was often the result of a minor mistake, which would prompt their supervisor to wreak havoc among the rest so that they would work at a high speed without making mistakes—once beaten, twice shy was the policy in practice. Beatings were a ritual, those who shouted during it got more beaten up. This was a rule to be strictly followed while undergoing the daily ritual since the factory was in a residential area. Also, a high-volume music system would be on to drown the cries. They were forced to completely accept the bondage. After this stage, the children would start behaving like robots.

Days started early in the morning and ended late into the night without any break for rest, food was scarce and a little water was available. It was the time when the temperature in Jaipur hovered around 44–46 degrees Celsius. All the children felt shackled, they were sleep-deprived, had no contact with their families despite their repeated requests, physically bonded and emotionally shattered with no escape in sight. What horrified them was sitting 16 hours a day on their knees, and the sight of children as young as seven years old working with their nimble, injured fingers all the time.

These eight children were facing many issues but the most difficult one was to sit on the floor as per the usual schedule, work started around 7 am and continued till 11 pm. The new cluster of children would be exhausted by 6 pm, whereas the other group of children who had been working there for months would work up to 11 pm without blinking their eyes. However, they also had to go through severe beatings for minor mistakes. The cuts, injuries, fever, headache and sickness were completely ignored.

There was an order from one of the regular customers for a huge quantity of bangles for a marriage ceremony. A deal was struck with the customer. This deal made the lives of the children a living hell as they had to work continuously for three days without sleep. Chilli powder was sprinkled on their eyes to wake them up from drowsiness triggered by the sleepless nights.

If a bangle broke while working, the supervisor would puncture their body with the broken end of the bangle. It was excruciating for both the boy who was undergoing the torture and for the rest who were made to feel the pain of what he was going through, they could be the next victim any moment. It was a daily ritual. The puncture marks were visible on their bodies.

Their hopes for a better future had turned into a nightmare. Liberty, freedom and play had become a thing of the past. The scenes of playgrounds, faces of friends and relatives, kept their minds occupied. Their native cuisine, especially rice and items prepared with rice, was missed all the time. Ashish missed his village school a lot. His dream of getting quality education in a private school had turned into a nightmare.

Ashish's mother would call the number given by Sikander multiple times a day. The phone was in switched-on mode only for a couple of days, it kept ringing, but went unanswered.

There had been no conversation between the mother and the son, since the day they left for Jaipur. Trying the same number every day became a part of her life.

Two months on, all the parents were worried and talking frequently among themselves about their children. They were apprehensive that something was amiss and that they had been cheated. They started looking for the child trafficker, who had given them an address from a nearby village. All the parents together visited the village, but they were shocked to know that no such person lived there. The search spread to other villages in the district and went on for months. They met with no success.

The news of children being taken to Jaipur, by some strange fellow in the name of employment and guarantee of a good education, and families losing connections with children thereafter had spread like wildfire in the nearby areas.

A social worker, Deena Nath Maurya, who worked at the district level in the area of child protection, happened to be in the village and came to know about the incident. He met the families and told them that their children might have been trafficked into the bangle-making factories in Jaipur where children were in huge demand to produce high-quality bangles with their nimble fingers. He told them that hundreds of children from Gaya district had been trafficked to Jaipur to work in the bangle factories. "Immediately lodge a complaint with the police station, with all the details about the children," said the social worker while kickstarting his motorcycle to move on to another village.

In the evening, the parents had a meeting on the advice given by the social worker—about complaining at the police station. However, they were not able to understand the meaning of the term used - child trafficking. There were mixed opinions. At last, they decided to go to the police station. The very next day, they went to the nearby police station. They reached the premises but did not have enough courage to go inside. They came back without filing a missing person report.

With every passing day, Ashish's mother was breaking down and slipping into severe depression. She would cry inconsolably, and tell her husband to go alone to the police station and lodge a complaint about the trafficked children as other parents were reluctant in reaching out to the police.

Back in Jaipur, Rakesh was getting beaten up more frequently than the others since he was finding it difficult to adjust to the labour. His seasoning period had been prolonged in comparison to others. One day, late into the night, he broke open the window when everyone else was in a deep sleep, and jumped out of the first-floor window onto the ground. There was a heavy thud and it woke many from their deep slumber. Ashish woke up due to the noise, went to the toilet, and came back to his sleeping spot—which had just enough space for him to lie on his side. He slept without realising that one of his close friends had broken the shackles of bondage and walked freely.

The following morning, the rest had to undergo severe beatings for not waking up the supervisor when Rakesh broke open the window. The children were traumatised by the abuse and nursed visible injuries on their faces and all over their bodies. Ashish lost his good friend and was also beaten badly. While he was learning to live without a good friend, far away from his family, he befriended Rahul who was also trafficked from Gaya, but from a different location far away from his home village. Soon, the friendship between the two grew stronger. Although Rahul was pensive and restless when working, his mind was always roaming free in the world, beyond the factory's four walls and the constant annoying sounds of the bangle-making process. They spent their days completing their duties, in a room filled with work noises so that they had to speak loudly to make themselves heard.

One afternoon, the ustad (supervisor) asked Rahul to get him a cigarette. He received a ten-rupee note and stepped out of the room. He was out in the open, he walked a few steps slowly towards the cigarette shop, but he passed through the shop and started running at a speed that would win any sprinter a gold medal in the Olympics.

Minutes after that the ustad became worried about Rahul. He went outside and walked to the shop and started looking for him. He walked through the market but could not find Rahul. Soon he realised that Rahul had escaped. In no time many motorcycle-borne men ran went in different directions, but no one could catch Rahul. He was lucky. He somehow reached a police station. Huffing and coughing, he narrated everything to the police in one breath.

The End of the Terror

Hours later into the evening, a raid was conducted in the factory premises by a posse of police; Rahul was also with them guiding to the factory in the multi-storeyed building. The children working in the room did not realise what was going on and some of them started shivering with fear as the traffickers had told them that the police would put them in jail for not working properly. Soon, the social workers present in the team sensed that the children were scared and reassured them the police were there to save them. Six children were rescued, the rest were taken out of the factories by the traffickers through the doors at the back of the building. The rescued children looked emotionless, malnourished and exhausted, and two of them were barely able to stand on their feet. The factory was sealed off. Two traffickers were arrested including the ustad.

Ashish stepped out of the factory after seven months of confinement. Some of the children were crying inconsolably out of their fear of the police, despite being repeatedly reassured by the members of the rescue team; their trust had been breached many a time before. Ashish managed to control himself, he managed to catch a reassuring nod from Rahul. Their rescue team consisted of the government child labour rescue team comprising officials from various departments and a couple of social workers. The rescued children sat in a vehicle and were offered water, while the traffickers were taken away by the police in another. There was silence since the children had no idea of what would happen to them next.

Soon they reached the police station. They were comforted by the police. They spoke fearlessly against the traffickers and about the ordeal. The presence of their assaulters did not deter them from revealing the truth, however, some of the children were still sobbing. They were then asked to sign a few papers. A First Information Report (FIR) was lodged against the employer and the trafficker, and both of them were booked under Section 370 of the Indian Penal Code (IPC), which defines the offence of human trafficking, among many other relevant sections. There had been very recent changes made in the law following the Nirbhaya case, the infamous Delhi gang rape and murder, that armed the criminal laws with stringent provisions to punish human traffickers.

Even though Article 23 of the Constitution of India prohibits human trafficking, it took the lawmakers of the country around seven decades to codify the crime.

All the rescued children were traumatised deeply, not knowing what was in store for them. The police rescue had been sudden and had given them no time to collect their belongings.

On the way, the children were counselled by social workers and other officials who informed them that they had been freed from the clutches of the traffickers who would be punished for committing the crime.

Why do these children end up in such situations? *Garib ka bacha, kamayega nahin toh khayega kya* (If the children of the poor do not work, how will they survive). But going deep down into it, I strongly feel that these children are targeted by certain sectors that stand to make more profit by employing kids rather than adults.

Child trafficking is largely a demand-driven problem. The demand is generated by industries that exploit children. Their short heights make them a good fit for labour in cotton farms, their agility makes them ideal workers in small dhabas and hotels, and their nimble fingers are in demand in bangle factories to produce good quality bangles at high speed.

Dreams of good quality education and a good life made them victims of such extreme situations. Ashish had always wanted to go to a convent school for quality education, and this had been used to lure him into accepting the work in Jaipur, which then put an end to his school education.

The pain and deprivation that they had gone through were irreparable and would impact them negatively throughout their lives. They had become much older than their ages.

The whole process took hours; they had food and water at the police station. They were experiencing for the first time in their life that the police helped in times of crisis, and it was debunking the age-old myth prevalent in underprivileged classes that the police did more bad than good.

A battery of journalists and television cameras suddenly appeared and started clicking photos and recording videos. This was all new for the children.

The rescued children did not understand why they were being photographed, recorded and asked to speak about their experience. Many journalists were speaking a mix of Hindi and English. Some of the questions got the Magahi speaking children completely confused, so they could not answer most of the questions. They realised that child labour was an offence, even if it was done with the consent of their parents.

However, the police cautioned them not to divulge much information. The Juvenile Justice Act (JJ Act) - 2015, strictly prohibits newspapers, magazines and other media from making reports that may lead to the identification of the child victim. These provisions are indicators of the progressive laws enacted in our country to protect the rights of children.

Late into the night, they were produced before the Child Welfare Committee, Jaipur, which ordered them to stay temporarily at a children's home. They could go back to their homes only after the completion of procedures laid down in the JJ Act, a relatively new dedicated legislation that has been enacted following international tenets promoting child rights in the country.

All children were pleading with folded hands to be sent directly to their homes in Bihar, but to no avail. The rescued children fall under the category of 'child in need of care and protection' as defined by the act. The act stipulates a set of procedures to be strictly followed in administering the decisions, keeping in mind the best interest of the child—one of the core guiding principles of the act.

The JJ Act, a very progressive legislation, has its genesis in the protection of child rights that was adopted by the country in 1992, and over the span of 30 years, it had undergone many changes, more than any other law in the country. The country has been positioning itself to a new set of laws that are aimed to better protect children. The whole legal system along with other institutions is trying to adopt the changes.

The JJ Act defines a child in need of care and protection based on their conditions and circumstances, and child labour is one of them. It also lays out a series of rehabilitation measures to be taken by the stakeholders, keeping in mind the developmental and other associated needs of children. It also refers to the role of stakeholders including the police and the media. The need for confidentiality of children's records is also reiterated.

When the children were asked to sit in a vehicle, Ashish wanted to know where his rescuers were taking him. He wanted to go home. He was told that he was being taken to a children's home. Ashish did not know what a children's home was, but he did not ask any further questions.

Soon, they reached a building and were asked to get down from the vehicle. Ashish was hesitant before entering the premises. It looked like a jail to him. The trauma of being controlled violently in the factory was still visible on his face. He hesitated a bit before entering the building.

Life at the Children's Home

Ashish entered the children's home with others, he thought that he would be staying there just for the night before going to his native place—Gaya.

Children's homes mainly look after orphans, who have been abandoned or surrendered, and survivors of neglect, abuse, violence, and trafficking, under the age of 18. There are broadly twelve categories of such children facing difficult circumstances. They are grouped under the Child in Need of Care and Protection (CNCP) category. Children's homes under the Juvenile Justice System run on the principle of institutionalisation as a measure of last resort.

Children's homes in India are run by both charity organisations and the government and have to be registered under the JJ Act. The number of children's homes in the country jumped manyfold following a flagship child protection scheme—Integrated Child Protection Scheme (ICPS) 2009—launched by the Ministry of Women and Child.

The ICPS provides shelter for children who fall under the CNCP category.

At the children's home in Jaipur, Ashish and other children received holistic care, which included safe living accommodation, nutritionally balanced food, constant health care, recreational and cultural activities, counselling, personality development, mentoring, life-coping skills and quality education along with uniforms, clothes, and books as per the provisions of the Juvenile Justice Act, 2015.

The children's home had a homely atmosphere with good facilities. Most importantly, the children received much-needed love and care from trained home staff who cared for the children as their own. The staff was trained to ensure high standards of care for the children.

At the children's home, all seven children were given separate beds in a hall with some other children who had been residing there for months. The children's home had a routine that was followed by each child. Their day started with yoga and exercises, followed by breakfast. They were grouped for study according to their education level. The new entrants took time to follow the routine properly. The children who had been residing in the children's home for months did not become friends immediately with the new entrants, making them feel uncomfortable.

Meanwhile, the children were receiving counselling. Their home addresses were also taken from them. This was the first step towards going home. The addresses were further verified by their native states. Six of the seven children gave their address correctly, whereas the seventh child did not. It took the counsellor more than a week to get the child to share his correct address.

He was angry and in pain, and needed immediate psychological help. It looked like their childhood was completely robbed, and their lives would not be the same again.

Children rescued by the police are taken to children's homes but with little psychological support in place, they usually refuse to open up to the staff, police, media or lawyers. Ashish was also withdrawn, in shock, and frightened. His body and mind needed immediate psychological help.

The children's home functionaries took them to a nearby government hospital for medical check-ups. After a couple of visits and agonising wait of long hours, the medical check-ups were finally done. All of them, except Ashish, were found free of any major diseases.

Ashish befriended some of the boys who had been in the children's home for some months. He asked one of the boys why he was there for so long. "I remember I was much younger when my mother who had been bedridden and suffering from cancer passed away. My father married another woman soon after the death of my mother. My new mother did not like me, she used to keep me hungry, and beat me badly whenever I expected my father to hug me and love me. I left home, spent days on the streets, and brought here by a social worker. It felt bad to live here in the beginning, without my father who I loved a lot. Slowly, I learned to live without him", stated the 15-year-old boy while expressing his grief.

"My father was an alcoholic and passed away. My mother married another man and left me on the streets. Since starting, the idea of living here seemed weird to me but I had no choice", said another 13-year-old boy. Before joining this children's home, "I used to live on the streets, depressed and scared. I was sexually abused every night in return for food until a charity organisation rescued me and shifted here. After coming here, I never had to stress about fulfilling my daily necessities. I am pleased how my life has changed," said another 14-year-old boy. He attended a nearby government school with the hope of becoming a lawyer when he grew up.

Symptoms of deteriorating mental health do not get priority in children's homes except in cases where the child behaves violently or hurts others, including the functionaries of the institute, only then the matter becomes serious, and the child receives medical care.

The rescued children kept asking the functionaries if they could go home. They did not want to stay at the children's home anymore.

Ashish noticed that some children were fully adjusted to their lives within the children's home; following all the routines from waking up early to going to schools outside the children's home and playing both indoor and outdoor games upon returning from school. Whereas some children aged 7–10 would cry inconsolably, asking to go home. He came to know that some of them had lost their parents, and their extended families were not ready to accept them. In some cases, their families' whereabouts were not known.

Most of the rescued children showed problems with behaviour and detachment. They were shy and reluctant to interact and express themselves. Others reported that they refrained from interacting with outsiders because they didn't know what to say.

While working at the factory, Ashish had inhaled a lot of chemical dust, which was used for laying and fixing nudges on the bangles, and it had clogged his lungs. Ashish had been feeling restless for a little over a month. His doctor advised him to immediately undergo a minor surgical operation for removing the dust from his lungs. He underwent a surgical operation at the hospital and felt much better afterward.

The CWC judged that the children had been working as bonded labourers and produced them before the Sub-Divisional Magistrate (SDM). The SDM interacted with the rescued children who narrated to him their working conditions and how their parents were given two thousand rupees and a verbal agreement of work before being brought to Jaipur. The children were confined in a small room and made to work 15–16 hours a day on a frugal diet. Communication with their families was not allowed, even over the phone. The traffickers forfeited their freedom of movement and left no scope for changing the employer, or the workplace. If the parents called frantically to talk to their child, the traffickers arranged a call after a series of warnings to the child: "Say that you are alright here and that there is no difficulty at all."

In a couple of days, they all received certificates—bonded labour release certificate—declaring that they were no longer under bondage, and any advance made by the employer to render labour stood settled. This certificate could get them on the fast track to economic rehabilitation. Which in turn would help them claim their entitlements under special welfare schemes such as the Central Sector Scheme for Rehabilitation of Bonded Labourer - 2016. This is a scheme that provides financial assistance of three lakh rupees to rescued children. The financial assistance for rehabilitation is fully funded by the central government. The release of rehabilitation assistance is linked with the conviction of the accused. However, immediate assistance of up to twenty thousand rupees may be provided to the rescued bonded labour by the district administration irrespective of the status of conviction.

The certificates were collected from the children and kept safely in the secretariat of the CWC. It would be handed over to the officials representing Bihar, who would then use these certificates to ensure that the entitlements reached the children on time.

After three months, a total of 46 children, all rescued in multiple phases from bangle factories located across Rajasthan, boarded a Gaya-bound train. A general compartment was reserved for them. There were police escorts all around. By now, staying close to government officials, including the police, did not perplex them much. They saw many people around them exchanging papers, giving directions and suggestions to the team members. They had to wait at the station as the train was late by four hours.

The four hours went by, the train arrived and they boarded and occupied their spaces. There was a flash of happiness in going back home after months of agonising wait. Even though the provisions of the Juvenile Justice Act talk about the best interest of the child, it took months to complete the formalities to send them home.

There were some government officials, a few social workers, and police in the compartment. No other passengers were allowed in that coach. All the doors were locked from inside by the police who kept a constant watch on the children. They were ready to thwart any attempts to run away from the moving train. A head count was done every three to four hours. The children in general were silent throughout their journey. However, they made small groups and talked among themselves. Most of them appeared stoic and serious. The process of being trafficked, the torture of various kinds at the factory, and the rescue and related time-consuming process had made them hopeless.

The next morning, they arrived at Gaya. The children were received by the government officials.

Having received word that their children were coming to Gaya, many parents had reached the station a day before to hug and receive their children.

But they could only see and talk very little to them as they were under the protective custody of the Juvenile Justice System. The children moved on to a waiting bus parked outside of the railway station along with a group of police officers who were deputed to avoid any untoward situation. But the sight of the children after months relieved the parents a lot.

They boarded the bus parked outside the railway station and reached the children's home. There were some officials from two government departments. The Labour Resources Department and the Department of Social Welfare are the two main departments that work towards preventing, combating and eliminating child labour in the state.

At the children's home in Gaya, they had to complete all the processes they had gone through in Jaipur: appearing before the CWC, staying at the home and following their routine, undergoing medical check-ups, etc.

The following day, the news of the return of all 46 survivors of child trafficking got prominently covered in the print media, along with the children's blurred photos. It helped alert the senior officials and the general public that child trafficking still existed in the district, and it exists in a big way.

The children stayed at the home for a little less than a month, while the CWC completed some procedures with the District Child Protection Unit—a government institution that works for child protection in the district, with the support of some charity organisations. The protection unit extends support in addressing the verification process and also assists in preparing the Social investigation Report (SIR)—a seven-page long format that records all information related to the child. It is on the basis of the SIR that the CWC makes decisions keeping in mind the best interest of the child, one of the core guiding principles of the JJ Act.

The children were desperate to go to their villages. The confinement at the factory, and then protective custody at the children's home in Jaipur and again in their native district, Gaya, made them feel low and dull.

They were restless inside the building. Many of them could not understand why they were in a somewhat jail-like environment for months for an offence committed upon them by the child traffickers. They wanted to step out, but they could not, for reasons beyond their control.

At the children's home, they were registered to generate an Aadhaar number. Bank accounts were opened in each of their names so that they could receive monetary assistance from the government in the shortest possible time. The process gave them hope for some monetary support. It was a silver lining amidst all the gloom.

The parents came to the children's home with some homemade sweets to feed their children but were not permitted to see their children or spend some time with them. They asked a number of questions to the guard, who was in the police constable uniform, sitting at the gate of the home. "Go to the CWC that convenes three days a week, go see them," said the constable. "When the child will step out of the children's home is always decided by them, we cannot help you on this front," he added. That day the CWC did not convene to do any business. And, the distance between the CWC and Ashish's home was 40 km. The parents went back to their village questioning the delay for nothing.

The trips from the village to the city and back home were expensive for these families: the travel costs plus expenditure on food and loss of wage for a day. They went back empty-handed without having spent any time with their children but had got a fixed date for the release of their children. Nonetheless, the children explained the procedures to their parents and also added that they would receive monetary support from the government. How much support would be given was the most discussed question among parents, and they asked many people about it but did not get any coherent answers. But, they went with a strong hope for a better future ahead.

The child and the parents both wondered about the procedures and failed to understand why it was happening to them or how it would affect their lives once the child was reunited with the families.

Ashish who took time to be friendly, slowly interacted with some of the children who had been residing in the children's home for a long time. A 12-year-old boy who lost both his parents in a short span of time and had lived in the children's home for over four years said, "I am happy to be here because now I can fulfil my basic needs. I get to eat on a daily basis. I don't have to sleep hungry anymore or fend for myself on the streets, without proper clothing. Now I can sleep well without having to worry about the food for the next day."

Ashish told me that most of them were lonely and often felt hopeless. Two boys (11-year-old and 13-year-old) stated, "We feel we are a burden on others. Nobody is interested to know how our day at school was or how we are feeling." Other children shared similar opinions, "We have nobody to share our feelings. We cannot tell the staff at home; they might feel offended. There is nothing to hold on to or something that is our own; sometimes life doesn't seem worthwhile." On the contrary, there were children who enjoyed being with other children and poured their hearts out to them.

"Whenever I see a child with his mother, it reminds me of mine, and I wish my parents were still alive. Sometimes I wonder why God did this to me," stated a 10-year-old child. Another 11-year-old boy reminisced, "I often see them in dreams. Their (parent's) thoughts keep hounding me so I cannot sleep peacefully."

"I feel jealous of my classmates staying with their parents. I always wish there could be some secret magic to bring back my mother. I miss my parents," told a sobbing 11- year-old boy. On the other hand, the older children were still a little satisfied because the other children had become their family and they cared for each other. A 13-year-old mentioned, "I am thankful that I got to live here, at least I am not roaming the streets. I have made many good friends here, and now this is my only family."

Most of the children stated, "Our classmates are afraid of us because we stay in the children's home and go together to the school. So, the children at school think we live in a prison and that if they talk to us, they will become imprisoned too." Many children reported their concerns about whether they will be able to fit in the society or more so be accepted by society. Other children were afraid to voice out their opinions fearing embarrassment. "Whenever I gave my opinion on anything, I would be made fun of, and other children would laugh at me. Now I don't say anything at school to avoid embarrassment" pointed out a 13-year-old boy.

A 17-year-old child shared with Ashish, "Soon I'll be going out of the children's home, but I have nothing to secure my future, neither a good degree nor a job. Decent standards of living is a faraway dream, I fear that I'll not be able to secure daily necessities for myself." The children believed that their future was quite insecure and dark. They often felt there was no one to take care of them if something went wrong.

Most of the rescued children had behavioural and detachment problems. They were shy, less interactive and expressive compared to others. A 13-year-old 'child trafficking survivor' mentioned how he felt shy to interact with strangers, "I mostly prefer to interact with someone like me (child trafficking survivor). I feel uncomfortable while talking to other children at school. I feel they will make fun of me." "Whenever I gave my opinion on anything, I would be made fun of, and other children would laugh at me. Now I don't express myself at class to avoid embarrassment," pointed out a another 14-year-old child trafficking survivor. Others reported that they refrained from interacting with strangers because they didn't know what to say and were hesitant to put forth their opinions. Attachment disorders were also noticed among the survivors. "I don't like to hug anyone and also don't like it when anyone touches me. I don't like to mingle with anyone on the go, because we mostly had to interact with many agencies after being rescued," Rahul told. Although most of the survivors reported that they were comfortable with the children at their children's homes, but avoided mingling with newcomers.

Many questions ran through their minds but one thing was sure, many of them called the children's home in the villages as children's jail and the rescue operation was termed as arrest by the government. They wondered why all this happened to them for the wrongs committed by the traffickers. They told themselves that this happened because they were very poor.

Reunion with Families

The local traffickers stay in touch with the network of employers who prefer to re-traffic rescued children as they already have the necessary skills required for work.

Meanwhile, Sikander—the henchman for the local child trafficker—also made incognito visits to the children's home to keep a tab on when they would be released from there. He had made a few visits to their native villages and had met with their parents to discuss taking them back to factories after their reunification with families. Although this offer was rejected outright by the parents, they were promised regular payments of five thousand rupees.

After four weeks, the parents were informed that they could go to the CWC with their identity cards to receive the children. They became happy and went ahead as suggested.

This time the traffickers tried to forge documents of consent from parents who were working in different states. They would use this to access the children in the shelter homes.

I met Mantu Kumar Vimal, a social worker in Muzaffarpur, who works in the field of child protection, and is rebuilding the lives of child trafficking survivors who were rescued from bangle factories in Rajasthan. He said that while doing outreach to the rescued children who were said to have been reunited with their families, the given address never existed in reality. The mobile phone numbers written on the documents were of somebody else. "I tried a lot to find them but I could not reach out to some of the children. They might have been received by traffickers who posed as the parent before the CWC, to take back the skilled children. The rescued children were trafficked by the same traffickers, applying a different modus operandi," said Vimal, expressing anger and sadness.

At the CWC secretariat, there was a huge crowd comprising of parents, lawyers, social workers and family members as many other children were being released. Ashish's mother was making sure that she had brought all the necessary documents, and was desperately waiting for her turn. The clock was ticking slow, her number came quite late at 4 pm, she did all the procedures as asked, and assured the CWC verbally that she would not send her son to work before he turned 18. She got her son back! She embraced him and cried, but controlled herself immediately, and went home by auto, hired jointly with other parents.

They reached the far away village a bit late into the night.

When the children reached their homes, they were the centre of attraction and the talking point. Many people gathered around them and started asking many questions. The crowd was growing thicker.

We read about you in the newspapers last month. Were you in jail? What was the daily routine to follow? Were you beaten? What did you do during the last 30 days? Why weren't you allowed to come home immediately? What was the point of keeping you in a children's home in your native district? How was the food there? Were you served khichari frequently?

The children were always surrounded by fellow villagers. They had to describe their ordeal over and over again. And the same questions were thrown at them.

Subsequently, all the children started staying at home, to avoid such questions. They started withdrawing themselves from their community.

The whole episode affected them deeply and made them dull, disinterested and distracted. It completely drained them from inside. They were back in their native places but they felt like they were still in captivity. The ordeal that they had gone through and the insensitiveness of the community people in their village had become a constant headache in many ways. Many thoughts were running through their minds: why are people behaving like this to us. What crime did we commit? These questions brought back painful memories, which they wanted to forget. They battled the stigma of being child trafficking survivors in their community.

Ashish went to his school and requested the teacher for re-admission. He was re-admitted and resumed his study. Although he had lost a year, he soon became popular in his new class. In a short time, he became dear to all the teachers in his school, especially the Hindi teacher as he loved the subject most.

Everyone in the village was talking about the financial support that they would receive from the government, but no one was sure about the amount or when it would reach them. Why were they being paid? What purpose would that serve?

Few in the village were aware of the fact that the children were rescued from a factory because they were all below 14 years of age and that it is prohibited by the specific laws in the country and is treated as a cognisable offence. And, that rescue is different from arrest and the children's home is not a jail.

Child trafficking is an organised crime. Despite being illegal, forced and bonded child labour is widespread. Child traffickers flout the law with impunity and there is limited legal recourse for victims. Bihar is the home to an estimated 10.88 lakh victims of child labour. The district of Gaya has the highest number of child labourers. It is around 78,929, according to the Census 2011.

Re-Trafficking Attempts

Just after Holi in 2018, another local trafficker was trying to trap three children all aged between 9–12, from the same village. The illiterate and landless parents had received an advance of three thousand rupees each, a week before Holi, on an agreement that the kids would join work in a roadside dhabha near Grand Trunk Road in the neighbouring district of Rohtas.

The trafficker arrived in a sports utility vehicle, Scorpio, and two men alighted from it and went to the children's houses. In no time, the vehicle was surrounded by a huge crowd of community people, largely women and youth, who had arrived under the leadership of Ashish who had received a tip-off about the arrangement. He had formed a youth club to keep a watch out for suspicious activities related to child trafficking. A fierce war of words broke out between the community members, who were opposing the trafficking, and the parents who had struck a deal with the trafficker. The parents demanded: how are we to feed them if they don't work. They were unaware that the law does not empower parents to strike deals with traffickers or employers on behalf of children to deprive them of educational and developmental opportunities and to put them in exploitative working conditions in the name of poverty at home.

Meanwhile, Ashish made a call to the nodal officer of the District Anti-Human Trafficking Unit who alerted the local police station in Sherghati. They were asked to thwart the trafficking attempt and report back.

The traffickers, sensing that the situation had grown beyond their control, asked their driver to park their vehicle far away from the village and took the children through a narrow village route, which was in the opposite direction of the parked vehicle, to dodge the police. They had noticed Ashish receiving a call from the local police station, and that the caller on the other side was taking down real-time details. They knew that the police would reach the spot in a short time.

Soon the police arrived, many villagers who were opposing the trafficking left the spot slowly, for the fear of entangling in the matter. Ashish turned up to them and narrated the story, and showed them the direction in which the traffickers has set out with the children.

The Scorpio which was parked far away from the village saw the police and moved to a nearby crowded market.

Police rushed in that direction and walked about three kilometers, but could not track them down. They came back to the village and started asking the parents for details about the traffickers. The parents were completely unaware of their work location, so they could not give any details except a phone number that had been used for communication with the traffickers.

When the Child Welfare Police Officer—a designated police officer who exclusively deals with children, either as victims or perpetrators, in coordination with the police and voluntary organisations—made a call on the given number, the number was switched off.

The patrolling squad while returning to the police station brought the parents and some villagers who had spotted the Scorpio in the market. Police immediately surrounded the vehicle and seized the driver's mobile phone.

After two hours, two traffickers along with the three children arrived. The police intercepted and detained the traffickers and brought them to the police station. All the three children were rescued, and reunited with their families. What the children experienced during a few hours made them traumatised. They were trying hard to hold back their tears.

Both the traffickers were arrested, and released after the execution of a personal bond which stated that if the children were re-trafficked, they would have to face regular prosecution.

The charity organisation fighting child trafficking in the district had organised special police-community meetings on many occasions. They invited the child welfare police officer to communities where incidences of child trafficking were very high and also arranged visits for the community people to the police station to bridge communication gaps. A small survey among the family members of rescued child labourers revealed that people get scared in calling or visiting police stations even in emergencies. The training paid off well.

Ashish felt good as it was his first fight against child trafficking and he was able to successfully stop it, leveraging his contacts with law enforcement agencies, civil society organisations, and community members. But what made him happier than the sense of achievement was the fact that the three children were saved before their childhoods were robbed. After working and undergoing various kinds of torturing at the workplace, including sexual exploitation, children become emotionally drained. However, the few hours that they spent being the centre of the ordeal had scared the children. They resumed their regular activities only after weeks passed by.

A large number of child labourers were sent back home during the first nationwide lockdown in 2020. Post-lockdown, many inter-state luxury buses started coming into rural parts of Bihar and were transporting the children back to destination states like Rajasthan, Karnataka and Tamil Nadu. The child traffickers changed their modus operandi because the railways—the most preferred mode for trafficking children—restricted their services to curb the spread of COVID-19.

The Bihar government was alerted by some charity organisations about this new mode of transportation. A letter from the Additional Director General of Police, Weaker Sections —which was mandated to prevent human trafficking—was issued to every Superintendent of Police posted across the districts. They, in turn, alerted every police station to intercept such buses and charge the traffickers with the right sections of the anti-trafficking laws.

A few buses were intercepted. But the traffickers were one step ahead of the law enforcement agencies; they had forged Aadhaar cards showing that the children were above the age of 18, even though they looked younger. Many buses were intercepted and inspected. Children with

Aadhar cards showing them as adults were allowed to go, in the absence of any mechanism to check the validity of their identification card.

The Gaya police intercepted some inter-state luxury buses at the district border and rescued 17 children who were being taken to work in a bangle factory in Jaipur. The news of the police being alert at the checkposts spread like a wild fire among those who were trafficking children. They quickly changed their routes, switched to vehicles like Bolero, Scorpio and Innova, and started taking buses from their neighbouring district. All buses which came in were returned empty giving an impression that the inter-state buses were not trafficking children.

One more modus operandi developed during pandemic times was that children would be accompanied by both parents, giving the impression that the parents were going back to work. The parents returned by the same bus and another set of children with their parents would be ready in Gaya awaiting the bus. Meanwhile, rescue operations in Jaipur were also going on, many children who were rescued during the pandemic revealed how they were trafficked to dodge the prying eyes of the police, Childline and NGOs, and dropped off at the factories.

Re-trafficking is a major challenge in the fight against child trafficking. The trafficked children become skilled over time and become assets to the establishments that exploit their labour, that's why they become subject to re-trafficking after being rescued and reintegrated with their families. This happens in the absence of a strong protection mechanism. For instance, during the lockdown, Shailendra (name changed), a 12-year-old boy, was rescued from a bangle factory in Jaipur. While his elder brother Narendra (name changed), a 13-year-old, was hidden by the trafficker at the time of rescue. When Shailendra was reunited with his family in Gaya, he revealed the shocking nature of torture that he along with other children had gone through. "If we did not do the work properly, or accidentally broke a bangle, we were thrashed mercilessly. After long working hours, we would doze off late into the evening. Then chilli powder was sprinkled into our eyes. The music system kept in the room was switched on when we cried out loudly during beatings to drown out our voices so that no one could know what was happening in the factory." Narendra's ankle got twisted when he was hit with a heavy rod.

Within a week of being reunited with his family, the local trafficker arrived at their home asking for Shailendra, to take him back to the factory in Jaipur. This was vehemently opposed by his parents, and they insisted that Narendra be brought home. But the trafficker kept mounting immense pressure on them to send back Shailendra. They threatened to kill the elder child otherwise. The mother spoke with Priyanka Baranwal, a final year student of TISS- Mumbai, who was doing an internship with an organisation that was rebuilding the lives of over 500 child trafficking survivors in the district of Gaya. Priyanka took her to a nearby police station to lodge an FIR against the trafficker. The FIR was registered, and Narendra was brought back home by Gaya police in December 2020. Narendra was produced before a judicial magistrate to record his statement under section 164 of the Criminal Procedure Code.

A witness protection application was moved to the competent authority in the district. A letter from the District Prosecution Officer was issued to the Deputy Superintendent of Police (DySP) concerned, for preparing and submitting a threat analysis report. The report would deal with the seriousness and credibility of the perceived threat to the witness or his family members, and suggest specific witness protection measures. After the wait of a month, a second letter was issued to the DySP, but the child witness and his family members were not approached even after the passing of several months. The family remains vulnerable to the traffickers. They feel scared. I met Narendra at his home. I tried to have conversations with him about his life at the factory and his plan for his life ahead. He was completely silent. He communicated with me only by telling 'yes' or 'no' or nodding his head.

The torture he faced for over two years was writ large on his face. He was completely malnourished and limping. "He stays inside the house and does not interact even with his childhood friends," said his mother holding her tears back. He had been robbed of his childhood.

However, Shailendra goes to school happily and spends time with his friends and plays cricket in the evening. He is good at maths. He wants to become a police officer.

Dhiraj Kumar, a 12-year-old from Dula Bigha, Tekari, was trapped by a local trafficker to work in a bangle factory in Jaipur inlate 2018. The trafficker had made an advance of five thousand rupees to his mother when his father was away. He along with two other children ended up in a small bangle factory in Jaipur, which already had five child labourers.

Trafficking of Children | 51

The owner of this factory was the same person who had trafficked Dhiraj from his family in Gaya. He was forced to work right from early morning 6 am till 9 pm, with only a short break to have lunch. Time went by, a raid was mounted by police and three children including Dhiraj were rescued. An FIR was lodged with Bhatta Basti police station in Jaipur.

Two years later, he was served a summons by Jaipur Police to appear on a given date, to record their testimonies. This alerted the local trafficker, who started mounting pressure on him to come back to Jaipur and speak in their favour. Otherwise, the advance given to his mother would have to be repaid, they said. The trafficker was mounting pressure, so his father, a daily wage labourer, informed the social worker of a voluntary organisation that was assisting Dhiraj to fight back against re-trafficking.

The social worker told the family to go to the police station and lodge a complaint against the trafficker. But when they approached the police station with a complaint, it was turned down and they were told to return the advance which was received two years ago. The social worker told the police officer that an advance in any form, whether cash or kind, in exchange for labour that would forfeit freedom of employment and the right to move freely is the prime element of bonded labour. They also went on to inform the police that the local trafficker must face legal action under the Bonded Labour Prevention Act, 1976. But the suggestion fell on deaf ears.

The voluntary organisation's top official shared the news with the senior-most anti-trafficking nodal police officer in the state who took it very seriously and wrote a letter to the senior superintendent of police to look into the matter, and to make sure that an FIR was lodged against the local trafficker and to report back with all details. The local Police took action against the accused.

2

Prosecution of the Child Traffickers

After two-and-a-half years, a summons issued by a Jaipur court was served to Ashish Kumar and three others in his village. The community members read it, and with their little legal knowledge came up with many interpretations. But the very next day with the support of a local lawyer, it became clear that it was a summons by the Jaipur court, mandating that the recipient—child trafficking survivors, now prosecution witnesses—had to appear in the court to record their testimonies in connection with the rescue operation and subsequent legal proceedings. A friend of the alleged trafficker approached them and offered ten thousand rupees to each of the parents. The offer was initially outright denied. Yet one of the parents could not resist their temptation and accepted the money in return for speaking in favour of the trafficker. The parent would have to testify that their child had been studying in Jaipur, not working.

There was constant pressure on the parents through influential people of that locality to settle the matter in the village by accepting the promised amount. After days of persuasion by the community, the parents appeared convinced and decided not to speak against the traffickers in the designated court in Jaipur. A charity organisation working in that area approached them and convinced them to testify in court since their children had undergone severe forms of exploitation, and were victims of an organised crime; they were encouraged to fight for justice.

The charity organisation had been re-building the lives of child trafficking survivors with a multi-pronged approach specifically designed to combat child labour; extending psycho-social support, providing educational bridge course,

Prosecution of the Child Traffickers | 55

re-enrolling them in school, extending necessary support so that they could continue their school, providing support to parents to raise their household incomes through micro-enterprises set up locally, and making them resilient enough to stop re-trafficking. They also formed formal and informal committees with the community people. The menace of child trafficking is symptomatic of a larger problem, but there is no denying the fact that it is fuelled by demand. Re-trafficking rates, fuelled by the demand for skilled children, are also high in the region.

After the rescued children are reunified with their families, traffickers approach families to take the child back to the factories. If families deny, all forces of various nature are applied to take the trained and seasoned children back to the factories

But now, the matter was with the court and listed for hearing, the children would have to appear for recording their testimonies as prosecution witnesses.

The same day late in the evening, a white SUV drew up near their homes. Six jeans-clad men with cotton *gamchas* around their necks got down from the vehicle, while three remained in the vehicle. They rushed to Ashish's house and called out his parents, in no time. Many community people surrounded them and more people kept coming, the six men singled out the relevant parents from the crowd, and intimidated and threatened them with dire consequences if they dared to go to the court on the given date. They saw the summons and threw it on their faces. They then got into the SUV and drove away through the narrow lanes of the village, leaving a cloud of dust behind. There was silence all around and people were looking at each other in utter dismay. Ashish's mother broke the silence by saying, "come what may, our child will go ahead with the case for obtaining justice." Soon, all the parents joined her in unison and reaffirmed their decision to fight against the injustice done to their children.

However, the parents of one of the children were aloof and said nothing about their decision. On the day they set out for testifying, they started looking for the child. His parents said that he had gone to his relative's home as one of their relatives had passed away.

As per the court mandate, the children, some of them accompanied by their parents, went to Jaipur, despite threats and intimidations from the local traffickers.

They boarded a Jaipur-bound train and sat in an unreserved compartment. The long journey started. They appeared worried. The children were anxious about speaking in court. Would the associates of the trafficker come to court with some goons to harm or prevent them from appearing in the court? A lot of things were running on their minds.

They arrived in Jaipur a day before the date. They spent some time at Hawa Mahal during the day. In the evening, their lawyers interacted with them, helped them recall and recount how they were trafficked and how they were forced to work for over 16 hours a day, in confinement without any contact with the outside world till they were rescued. The children were prepared for the difficult process of cross-examination. They had to give convincing testimonies in the witness box. Constant counselling was required to ensure the children were not intimidated in the witness box. They also had to be prevented from switching to the narrative that they had gone to Jaipur, along with their relatives, to study.

The next day they reached court early. Soon, the court sat, and the children were outside the courtroom where the matter was listed, waiting for their turn. Ashish suddenly saw the person who had abused him at the factory. The man approached them and threatened Ashish and others not to speak against the traffickers in the court. Ashish was freezing and started shivering in the scorching heat of Jaipur. A social worker sensed that something was amiss and took him and others to the lawyer's chambers. Ashish said that he saw one of his traffickers at the court and that they had been making eyes at him; threatening him not to go against them.

But the fortunes favoured the trafficker, the court could not carry out the proceedings as it was adjourned for some official reasons. All looked at each other in utter dismay and rushed to the station to catch a train back to Gaya

Their week-long efforts, energy, time and money were spent in vain; however, they got a new date for appearing in the court. The hearing would be after two months.

Back in the village, they narrated their experience of traveling to Jaipur with no outcome. "It happens in litigations," said the elders of the community, they were under influence of locally brewed alcohol, although liquor was banned in the state.

The children along with their parents had been advised against testifying by their fellow villagers. One fellow who was said to be very close to the accused, and who had tried persuading them not to go to the court in the Jaipur, was laughing at them uncontrollably, saying that he had got the date deferred. He started telling the parents not to listen to the charity workers, "just go to court and tell them that 'I went there for studying. I was there to study, not to work, I never worked." He also mounted pressure on the parents through influential people in the village to change their minds about obtaining justice in the case.

He said it was better to settle it in the village than go to the court. He hinted at payment if they agreed to turn hostile in court. Some of the parents appeared to have changed their minds about going ahead and obtaining justice.

Soon the local trafficker arrived and said, "you all have seen our power, we could defer even court dates." All those who had been to Jaipur just listened to him and tried convincing the others that he was lying. The trafficker added, "if you try to go there again, you will be killed," while crushing tobacco in his palms. After he went back, the parents apprised the local child protection organisation's representative about his arrival, utterances, threats and intimidation. They came to know that the traffickers had nothing to do with the postponement. The courts work at their own speed, with many halts. They would have to be ready for further delays if they wanted to obtain justice. Keep patience. The parents were relieved.

Time went by, they got to know the second date of their hearing and they needed to be there without fail if they wanted justice for the ordeal that they had gone through.

Again, after some in-person counselling by their local volunteer, they packed their bags and arrived in Jaipur by bus to avoid the traffickers.

Their lawyer was at the gate and after a brief exchange of greetings, they went inside the courtroom and sat for some time while other matters were being heard by the judge. All the survivors-turned-prosecution witnesses roamed their eyes around the court room. It was an entirely new experience for them, however, they had seen somewhat similar settings in movies. Soon, the name of a witness, Shibhu, was called out. Shibhu said that he had been hung upside down from a fan and beaten badly, several times, for being slow at work. The other three children were called to appear the very next day.

When Shibu came out of the room after recording his statements, the other three children surrounded him asking questions about the process, and what he had said. He narrated how he had spoken in the court room before the judge when he was prompted to speak about his experience after becoming the victim of child trafficking.

The next day, all the children assembled outside the court room, and went inside, one by one, when their name was called. They spoke about their ordeal, the modus operandi that had been used to cheat their parents through false promises, what they had gone through, and how they were deprived of their basic human rights during their confinement in the factories.

The judge was stunned listening to their experiences, her eyes revealed the pain she felt. The opposition lawyer who was defending the alleged child traffickers was advancing his arguments: the children had been brought to Jaipur with the consent of their parents. The judge replied that the consent of parents was immaterial in child trafficking.

The court master called the next case.

All the people related to the case, both prosecution and defence, stepped out of the court room. The defence lawyer soon became busy on his phone and was heard saying, "We could lose the case as all the children, except one, spoke against us. Pray to God."

One of the child witnesses who was slated to testify in the court was kidnapped two days before they were to set out for Jaipur. He was brought back home after the hearing. The others got to know of this only after they returned from the hearing. A similar incident had happened during the first date too. "We were all threatened with death if we went ahead and spoke against the traffickers," His mother narrated the story of how they were kidnapped and kept in an isolated home, in a village far away from their native village. "Two men came to our home in the wee hours and took all of us to a village, we were kept there for days and dropped back near the outskirts of our village at night. We were kept confined. So, we did not share the incident with anyone fearing danger to our lives."

Meanwhile, the parents and children who recorded their testimonies in court were facing constant threats from the accused trafficker. The parents along with their children were visibly worried and wondering what lay in the future for them. The parents hadn't gone to work for many days since they feared that the kids would be kidnapped.

After two months, one of the rescued children, Rahul, and his mother, and Ashish's mother were forcefully taken away in an SUV. They were taken to one of the local railway stations to board a train to Jaipur, and they were being persuaded to turn hostile in the court. They were scared of being held hostage, and apprehensive about their destination. Ashish's mother called the charity organisation's representative, who had been supporting them in their fight to obtain justice.

The charity organisation swung into action, made frenzied calls to the anti-human trafficking unit and the superintendent of police of the district. He responded quickly and immediately sent a team to the railway station to rescue the hostages. But the train had left the station. The next stop of the train was in another district. The jurisdiction of the district limited further interventions of the team.

The Additional Director General of Police, Crime Investigation Department (ADG-CID), in the state was informed. He was in Chandigarh, but was kind enough to pick up the call of a social worker, and alert the superintendent of Rohtas, the neighbouring district where the train was expected to arrive in an hour. The charity organisation's representative was put in touch with the SP. Multiple calls were frequently exchanged between them. Ashish's mother luckily had her tiny mobile phone fully charged, and was able to pass on information about their movements. She was receiving and making calls, surreptitiously hiding from the staring eyes of the thugs sitting in the same coach.

Meanwhile, the Rohtas police alerted all the stations where the train had stops and the traffickers could have potentially got down. But they had not. They were all in the train, sitting separately in the second last coach and on their way to Jaipur.

Soon the train arrived at the Dehri railway station, where they were spotted and rescued from the train. One of the trafficker's associates was also arrested, while the other accomplice got away.

An FIR was registered under all the relevant sections of the Indian Penal Code - 1860, against the two culprits. One of them was put in jail, while the police were searching for the other.

Those kidnapped were reunited with their families. It was a happy reunion at last.

Ashish who was home, and in the touch with the charity organisation throughout the rescue operation, was relieved when he heard that his mother and the rest were safely rescued by the police.

Seeing the kidnappers run away during the rescue reassured the villagers about the power of the police. They were now confident of approaching the police for help in times of emergency.

They appeared in the court the next day for recording their statement under Section 164 of the CrPC. The rescued child was the first to speak before the judge in the court room and he narrated everything in detail. The child trafficker-turned-kidnapper was denied bail and sent to jail.

The accused and the rescued child were from the same village. The rescued child had lost his father when he was 7 years old and came from a lower caste and did not possess even a small piece of land. All he had was a small hut that was vandalised by the family of the trafficker, who had been put behind the bars.

They were under constant threats from the accused, family and friends to turn hostile in the court even though the trial court had found the accused guilty of child trafficking. There was no respite for the parents or the children.

Every day the parents were being pressurised by local, influential people to assist the accused in getting bail and subsequent acquittal in the ongoing case.

Later in August 2019, the designated court in Jaipur pronounced its judgement. The alleged trafficker was sentenced to life imprisonment—it was the first time in the country that a child trafficker was being sentenced to the highest amount of punishment. History was being scripted, in tackling the organised crime of child trafficking through a successful prosecution. The Court also ordered that Rs. 1,46,000 be given as compensation by the convict, to be equally distributed among the four survivors who turned up in the court.

All the rescued children and their families celebrated the conviction, for them it was victory at the end of a long battle. The charity organisation that had been supporting the children and their families in the fight against the traffickers, for a little over three years, was in an upbeat mood. They were expecting many more convictions of child traffickers in the future.

But the happiness did not last for long.

The positive verdict in the case didn't bring any tangible aid to their lives, rather it made them more vulnerable than before, their fears were stronger than ever. The prime witness of the case and his widowed mother happened to live in a hut in front of the convict's house. They were ostracised by the village community. The mother was taunted for allowing her son to go to court for recording testimonies against their neighbour, who (they said) had been providing work and food for her child in the bangle factory in Jaipur. They had to spend many days without work despite having nothing to fall back on.

At last, they had to take shelter in a relative's house in another village. His mother who was the sole breadwinner had to shift to another village to find work. But they were hounded there too, by relatives and other anti-social elements for speaking up against trafficking and kidnapping. Fighting injustice amidst all the odds was an uphill task, but they never succumbed.

The aggrieved family was at last supported by the charity organisation that had supported them all through the trial in the court, and also when they were kidnapped by their neighbour-turned-trafficker.

The conviction rate in cases of child trafficking is woefully low in the country, despite it being an organised crime. It hasn't succeeded in making space on the agenda of law enforcement agencies with cases of murder, rape and sensational scams hogging all the limelight. The law enforcement agencies do not swing into action on their own. Justice is delivered only after charity organisations combating child trafficking assist the survivors in obtaining justice.

The convict then moved to the High Court, but was denied bail. After two years, the trafficker's family succeeded in getting parents of three children to sign an affidavit, which was submitted in the High Court, praying for the remand of the trial once again in the lower court.

Just after Holi in 2021, Ashish's mother was being pressurised by local politicians to sign the affidavit in line with the other parents. This would assist the convict in getting bail and subsequent acquittal. The family had been reeling under tremendous pressure and felt that they had no choice other than to succumb to the pressure, in one way or the other. But they kept fighting for justice for Ashish.

Child trafficking is purely a demand-driven problem. There are industries that need children to run efficiently and make more profits for owners. The bangle-making industry is one of them that needs the nimble fingers of children to produce fine quality bangles. There is also an economic factor, children are available cheaply and can be made to work 16 hours a day, every day of the week. They need less space to sit and sleep, and also do not need as much food as adults.

3

Dream of Clearing the Secondary Exam Comes True

Meanwhile, Ashish Kumar who had appeared for the secondary exam in 2021—popularly called matric in Bihar—was getting worried about his marks and division in the result. The date of the announcement of the result had been postponed by a week. Ashish could not attend regular classes in school during the 2020–2021 academic year due to the spread of COVID-19 and that had affected his studies a lot. Online classes were accessible only for wealthy students studying in private schools in urban and semi-urban areas. Poor students like Ashish, who studied in government schools, did not have the infrastructure to do so. He had to study at home by himself as there was no one educated enough in his community to teach him. He was worried about two papers—science and maths—but appeared quite confident about other subjects. And, Hindi was his favourite subject for which he was always confident of securing good marks.

The D-day arrived, the final date for declaring the matric results were decided and announced by the Bihar Board—the agency that conducts exams. It was to be announced at 3:30 pm on the given date. Ashish along with his mother went to a cyber cafe around 2:00 pm, it was 12 km away from his home. He submitted a photocopy of his admit card along with 40 rupees to the operator sitting in the cybercafe. There was a huge gathering of students and guardians outside the cybercafe, waiting anxiously for their results. The crowd was swelling. The admits cards were being collected in serial order. They were told that it was going to be done on a first-come, first-served basis. The clock struck 3:30 pm, and the operator started working on the computer. There was pin-drop silence for a moment as the operator announced that he was going to check the results. He clicked the link multiple times but was receiving an error message. He told the students to wait; the results would be declared soon. The website appeared to be not responding. Everyone present at the cybercafe got tense and frustrated about not being able to access the results at the given time. The crowd was growing thicker as time went by. Many were lining up to check their results. The operator was being showered with questions: What happened? How long will you take? Why are the toppers' names not displayed on the TV screen? Give our money back, we are going to another cybercafe.

There was complete chaos. Ashish and his mother were in the corner of the cafe just watching others react to the delay in results. Ashish looked at her mother, wondering what they could do. She told him to keep cool.

After an hour the website started responding, results were displayed as the operator entered various details into the website. The results were mixed: first division, second division, third division, failed and pending. Ashish was waiting for his turn, he asked the operator about his results, he was told to wait for five more minutes. Finally, it was Ashish's turn, he had secured second division. A printout of the result was handed over to him by the operator. Ashish cried with his mother over his achievement, he had become the first person in his big joint family to appear for and clear the matric exam. Both of them controlled themselves, and purchased some sweets from the market, and went back home. They distributed the sweets among the community people. There was a huge celebration in the community as he was the first in the community to pass the matric exam with second division.

There was a huge celebration among social workers of the charity organisation which supported Ashish in his pursuit of formal school education. His success in the matric exam, against all odds, was well received by the print media. He surfaced on the front page of the *Dainik Bhashkar* Gaya edition. Soon, he became a talking point for his struggle against all odds. The story of a victim-turned-survivor-turned-winner, and a source of inspiration for many. The local sitting Member of the Legislative Assembly of Sherghati, Gaya, visited his house to congratulate him over his success. She gifted him a few books and a pen. He was also invited by the Minister of Scheduled Caste and Scheduled Tribes Welfare, Santosh Kumar Suman, who congratulated and offered him all support to continue his education. Local officials and other elected representatives at the sub-division level also congratulated him. The visitors kept coming to his home for weeks to congratulate him, and to talk with him face-to-face even amidst the unrelenting surge in COVID-19 cases.

Ashish looked humbler than ever. He planned to study arts and was waiting for the situation to get back to normal. The rural areas were badly hit by the second wave of COVID, forcing the closure of schools and colleges for the second time.

Ashish went door-to-door requesting parents to send their children to school. He has enrolled over five hundred children in schools jumping on the bandwagon of the government enrolment drive after the second deadly wave of COVID-19 relented. He is part of a network that has united over 300 trafficking survivors rescued from across the country. Ashish works with a vision of transforming child trafficking survivors into thriving members of society. He interacts with survivors and lends feedback on how child trafficking can be eliminated in Bihar. He wants child trafficking survivors to be included in organisations fighting against the crime, and to participate in every committee that government forms. He wants them to float ideas to combat trafficking and believes that their lived experiences will always be a guide to draft strong anti-human trafficking policies. He says that a lot of anti-trafficking work is happening but the framing of policies and laws does not consider the survivor. This is one of the reasons we are failing to provide a holistic rehabilitation programme for the survivors of child trafficking.

He believes that educated survivors will lead the anti-child trafficking movement and create solutions for those rescued to grow in their lives. If provided with education, skills, leadership training and job opportunities, survivors will be able to transform their trauma into knowledge and expertise. He has also started a survivor-led organisation—VIJETA—to combat child labour and child trafficking in the state of Bihar.

He was chosen as the first runner-up in the Plan India Impact Awards- 2021, in the Best Young Changemaker (male) category.

4

Succumbing to Long Working Hours, Hunger and Lack of Medical Care

Rural areas in the state capital, Patna, are also not spared the menace of child trafficking. Eleven children from the Musahar community in Dhanarua block were trafficked in late 2017. It was a local trafficker who approached the parents of the children aged between 9–12 years. He offered the children work in a bangle factory in Jaipur; work for four hours a day, assuring their education and well-being. He promised that the children could come back to their village whenever they wished to, and their guardians would receive a sum of Rs. 4000 per month. The trafficker approached many parents with the same bait. However, only 11 parents accepted the offer. Three of them initially dillydallied, but accepted the offer when the other parents talked to them and advised them not to miss the golden opportunity for securing a good future for their children—decent work, education and wellbeing, what else did they dream of for their children. *It's a windfall, take advantage of it*, the trafficker said: *Opportunity seldom knocks twice.* While his eyes betrayed his tongue.

For Puniya Manjhi, it was a dream come true. He had always dreamed of educating his elder son so that he could spend his old age comfortably. He finally decided to allow his 9-year-old child to go to Jaipur. Their exact location was not known either to the parents or to their children. The night before their departure Puniya was sleepless, he hugged his child close to his chest, staring at the roof of the hut. The next day, they assembled at a predetermined location, carrying their essentials in a polybag. Many children were sobbing, there were intermittent high-pitched whimpering. The mothers were also crying while hugging their children. The fathers were also visibly sad but tried their best to control themselves. They had received Rs. 1000 each as a token amount for sending the children for work.

Soon a Patna-bound bus was flagged down. They were at the Dhanarua bus stop. They boarded the bus and reached Patna railway station after an hour. The following morning, they reached Delhi. They took a bus and reached their destination. It was a bangle factory with many other children already working there. Some of them seemed quite efficient at the work considering their tender age. The factory was buzzing with different sounds of the production activities.

All of the 11 children received work-related directions from a person who seemed to have a deep understanding of the work, then they were delegated work.

The children had to work at least 16 hours a day, there were no off-days. Initially, they missed their homes and wanted to talk to their parents, but no communication was allowed. Soon they stopped asking to call their families. However, their parents were still trying to reach them through a number given by the trafficker to no avail. The children were also traumatised by the separation from their families. Radhe Kumar, who was one of the trafficked children, was extremely worried when he saw that some of the children were crawling, and a few of them were walking with the support of the wall. And some of the younger children were not able to hold back their tears. They cried all the time.

Beating, bullying and hunger had become a normal affair. There were daily targets given to each child, and those who could not finish the work had to go to bed without food. Beatings with batons and electrical cables were common rituals for children who made mistakes time and again. Even those who requested rest or more food were also beaten, music was played at high volume to drown out the cries of the children.

Bits of broken bangles were punctured into their bodies as punishment for not completing the daily work, dozing off, or for breaking bangles while working.

Parents at home were worried and kept frantically calling the dealer who had approached them and assured them of assistance in case of any emergency. The parents hadn't received any money as promised. Months went by, and they grew anxious for their children. All they managed was to talk briefly with their kids over the phone, however, the children never spoke of what they were going through as there was always someone listening to their conversions. The parents were slightly satisfied with what they heard, as it did not seem that bad.

After a couple of months, Radhe Kumar started feeling stiffness in his knees. It was difficult for him to walk without any support. What he saw when he entered the factory had become the ugly reality of his life too. The long working hours spent seated on the floor had caused problems to their feet.

One of the injured children managed to run away from the factory and arrived back home, limping. He was shattered, broken and his body bore multiple bruises, inflicted by shards of bangles. He could not speak. His eyes spoke more than his words. He told the parents that he had been hit on his stomach with a baton by his employer, last week. He was soon taken to a nearby hospital that referred him to another hospital where he was admitted and given treatment.

After two days, when he felt better, he told his parents that he was beaten every day with sticks, rods, batons, electrical cable and belts. If he made a mistake at work, he was punctured with shards of bangles. None was spared the ordeal of beating, including the other children from his village.

This made the other parents worried. They cried inconsolably for their kids and tried calling on the number given to them. Amidst the flood of calls from parents, the number became unreachable. The worried parents grew impatient. They decided to visit Jaipur, even though they did not know the address. All the parents reached Jaipur. They were still trying the number which was intentionally switched off. They visited many places in Jaipur with bangle factories, such as Ramganj, Bhatta Basti, Galta Gate and Shastri Nagar. But all their efforts seemed to have failed. The worry grew stronger with each passing day.

However, the child who had managed to escape gave more information about their place of work, and it created a doubt that the children had been taken to Jaipur. The child said that he took a bus from his factory, and the bus took around an hour to reach New Delhi Railway Station so it meant he had been working in Delhi.

The good samaritans of the villages had met local officers, police and media persons seeking help to get back the children, but all in vain. *Hindustan* (a Hindi newspaper) published this news boldly, which brought the issue to the notice of Inspector General of Police – Weaker Sections. He directed the Senior Superintendent of Police to enquire into the matter and submit a report, but nothing happened. No efforts were made to find the children. I met Sarvesh Manjhi who lived in the same block and worked for the upliftment of vulnerable children. He worked with the Ambedkar Club that promoted the values of Baba Saheb Ambedkar among children. He too had visited the Dhanarua police station on many occasions, pleading to the officials to get the trafficked children back. The police had advised him to complain the absconding local trafficker who had played the role of the middle man. None of the parents, despite encouragement from fellow villagers, dared to lodge an FIR with the police station. They sensed that doing so would jeopardise the lives of their children who were already undergoing many troubles. The police remained inactive in this case. Meanwhile, the parents started mounting pressure on Uday Manjhi, a local trafficker. He was later killed in a road accident, giving rise to rumours that it was a murder planned by the main child trafficker. His death was interpreted by each individual differently. Was the accident intentional or not it remains unsolved.

After six months, another child from the same group came back home. But he did not come by himself. He was brought by the local trafficker. The local trafficker informed his parents that the boy had been unwell and not able to work, hence they were sending him back. The parents were asked to collect him from a spot that was five kilometres from their village. A call was made to the child's father to collect the child from the particular spot. When he reached the spot, he was shocked to see his child's condition. The kid was not able to stand on his feet. He was also badly bruised, with many marks on his body similar to the ones that the first boy had. These were wounds inflicted by shards of broken bangles. Some of them were quite deep and pus was coming out of them.

The child was deeply traumatised by the ordeal at the bangle factory and was dragging his feet with difficulty while walking. He had developed psychological disorders: difficulty in communication, dull face, and withdrawal tendencies. He slept most of the time and tried to hurt himself multiple times.

People from the whole village kept flocking to his home to know his wellbeing and would look at him with pity. Some of them cried, and some cursed the traffickers.

Many religious rituals were performed and his mother went on a fast for days, praying to God for his fast recovery. But he did not survive; he died. He breathed his last in the lap of his mother. He had constantly high fever for months while working in the factory. His illness was ignored and he was made to work for long hours, said another child who had come home.

His death sent out shock waves to the rest of the parents who had fallen into the trap of the traffickers. They kept cursing themselves for believing a bad local guy. What had they done to their children?

The rest of the parents whose children were stuck at work kept trying to know the well-being of their children over the phone. They did get connected with the children. But did not get to know what they were going through. All their dreams of having a regular monthly income were shattered, and so were the dreams of younger siblings who were eagerly waiting for many gifts to come from Jaipur—a city that was known for its elegant bangles. Of the eleven children, the last one came home after four-and-half years in September 2021. He said that the health of the children was deteriorating. As the health of the children deteriorated, and they become unable to produce bangles at high speed, they get replaced by newly trafficked children. The cycle of the exploitation of the underprivileged children, especially the Musahars, in the bangle factories goes on. Out of the 11 children, one died, one became silent and the rest are still struggling hard to come out of it emotionally. They are past their prime age to acquire a school education. Only three of them are going to school and they struggle a lot to match with the knowledge level of their peers. The rest of them are not willing to go to school. The vicious cycle of poverty seems to be continuing in the lives of these children.

Three child labourers from Bihar were reportedly found dead in the bangle factories when the country was placed under the historic 68-day-long nationwide lockdown to check the spread of highly contagious and then untreatable COVID-19. One of the dead child labourers was from Gaya.

Kunti Devi, 42, an illiterate widow was desperately searching for her youngest son Nishikant,13. Her son was trafficked while she was working in a paddy field in her village. Days turned into weeks; weeks turned into months. After seven months she received a call from Jaipur on a neighbour's number. The caller was a native of Gaya who was running a bangle factory in Jaipur. He connected Nishikant on the phone, who spoke to his mother and asked her not to worry. "I am fine and working at a factory. The workload is quite low, easy and adaptable. I work at night, and during the day I go to school," he said.

The mother knew that the children at bangle factories were treated badly and beaten severely for minor mistakes and she tried calling back on the same number several times but was never connected again.

After weeks, she received a call from another number. The caller was her son who tried comforting her, saying that he was doing all right. She kept asking about his wellbeing, with a doubt that he was being treated unfairly at the factories and made to work excessively long hours.

The communication was never free and uninterrupted, and she sensed that there was somebody constantly listening to the conversations. She believed that all was not well with her son, and that kept her worried. She requested the owner to take care of her son and he gave her his word.

She kept persuading and pleading with her son to come back home whenever she got connected. The mother was given multiple dates for his return, but with each passing day, her agony got stronger. The mother slipped into depression over the whole development.

She pleaded to the local trafficker to send back her son, but it fell on deaf ears.

A year after, COVID-19 broke out. The family again pleaded with the local trafficker-turned-factory-owner to return their child. "I heard about a disease which is killing many, and it has largely gripped the urban parts of the country. Please, please, send my child home. I heard that the government is imposing a lockdown for an indefinite period. How will my child survive the crisis?" The mother kept trying to get connected with her child, but all efforts went in vain.

In June 2020, it was around noon, when the mother received a call. It was a police officer from Jaipur who asked her to give the phone to a male member of the family. She gave the phone to her elder son Mithilesh, 22, who had been sitting next to her. The police asked him his connection to the lady, he replied that he was her elder son.

The police said that his younger brother had died in Jaipur. They asked him to come to Jaipur with a copy of Aadhar card, voter id, or any other identification document to collect the dead body. Mithilesh agreed to collect the body. In between, he tried asking many questions about how he had died, but the police did not give any further information.

The mother who was listening to the conversation started crying inconsolably at the end of the brief call. The elder son and his wife tried comforting the mother. Soon many people from the community joined them and tried to know what had gone wrong.

The bereaved family shared the incident and started asking for money so that they could bring back the dead body of her son. But no one lent them money.

The mother called the number back and said that she had been unable to arrange money. The police asked her to go to the nearest police station—Konch in Gaya—and submit an application expressing her inability to transport her dead son during the lockdown. She did that with an extremely heavy heart. She could not see the face of her son even after his death.

The mother did all the last rites with a symbolic human body made of paddy. She was supported by local leaders with strong words and little cash. She slipped into severe depression.

She was not the only one who had lost a child to the machinations of child trafficking.

Kanti Devi, from Korma village in Gaya, could have never foreseen losing her 11-year-old son to torture and neglect at a bangle factory. Hours of excruciating labour for months, after being trafficked on the false promise of a good life and an opportunity to continue education. In August 2020, her son was trafficked, along with five other children, by a local trafficker to a bangle factory in Jaipur.

Private luxury buses, with their tinted glasses, curtained windows and erratic time schedules had become the preferred mode of transportation for traffickers during the outbreak of COVID-19 since regular rail services had been cancelled. Traffickers quickly moved from trains to buses and found them a safer option, because it proved more difficult for activists and government agencies to conduct rescue missions.

Mohan was trafficked from his village Korma in Gaya to a bangle factory in a bus with dark windows. It was September 2020. Had Mohan not been trafficked, he would not have ended up with stiff legs and severe malnourishment. The pandemic-induced lockdown meant that schools were shut down and Mohan was home for months. The trafficker approached his mother with a job offer. "The job is a light one for which he will be paid well and also schooled during his stay. He will be given fruits and good food." The parents consented. They were not given the address of the factory. They just exchanged mobile phone numbers.

When Mohan arrived in Jaipur, he was made to work for 16–18 hours a day at a bangle factory, given food once a day and brutally thrashed for any mistake. There was hardly any communication between the mother and son. Neither parent received any monthly remuneration. When Mohan was rescued in March, his leg bones were fractured, and he was rushed to Anugrah Narayan Medical College and Hospital in Gaya. Doctors said that his organs were also failing due to lack of food, prolonged malnourishment and constant beatings. After four days of treatment, he was referred to Patna Medical College and Hospital. I met him there. He was crying in pain, and his mother was comforting him. His father was staring at the ceiling with little hope of his survival. Her mother was berating herself for believing a stranger.

Mohan was urinating in his bed, and vomiting even water. He was constantly shouting in pain. His lungs were completely damaged. He was discharged from the hospital after a week.

Mohan passed away in the last week of August 2021.

Just after four days, another child 14-year-old, Jacky Kumar, was received by his parents from the Jaipur Child Welfare Committee and brought back to the same hospital where Mohan had been admitted a couple of weeks ago.

Jacky Kumar who was also made to work 16–18 hours a day with little food, and minimal rest was suffering from severe tuberculosis and battling for his life. After two weeks in the hospital, he could pull through. He was at his home when I met him in the last week of September 2021.

After the Lockdown was Lifted

The lockdown was slowly eased in the following months. Small bangle factories were trying hard to come out of the financial losses triggered by the pandemic and subsequent lockdowns.

The bangle factories in Jaipur primarily rely on the nimble fingers of children to produce fine-quality bangles at no labour cost. They have to incur a one-time expenditure in bringing the children to factories. It costs them in the range of Rs. 7000–15000 per child. This includes a one-time payment to the parents of the child, which is around Rs. 2000-5000; transportation costs; and Rs. 5000 payment to the child trafficker. Rs.5000 is an average payment and it can be higher if the children come from very poor backgrounds; broken families; single-parent families; or is an orphan, which is the most sought after. These children can be easily forced to work 16–18 hours for as long as they stay healthy, as their families are rarely able to make an inquiry about the child or to push for a monthly payment through the trafficker.

The government through its ministries and affiliated institutions had issued multiple advisories alerting the state governments, through their chief secretaries, to step up the vigil against child trafficking.

The train services were not yet fully restored, and the general coaches were not attached to the handful of trains running at the time. The railway network is considered a cheap mode of travel by those who traffic children. And, transporting children in reserved coaches draws the attention of authorities.

Several child-rights activists, working in the state, who I spoke to said that it was an entirely new modulus operand. They said that an advisory was issued by the Additional Director General of Police alerting every district Superintendent of Police to thwart such attempts and to charge the traffickers under the relevant sections of the law. Subsequently, many inter-state luxury buses were intercepted by the police in some of the districts. A few of them were intercepted at the outskirts of Gaya. Some of the buses intercepted were full of children, but they had Aadhaar cards showing their ages as higher than eighteen.

The youngest child labourer that I came across was six-year-old Surendra Kumar, from Fatehpur Block, Gaya. He had lost his father when he was four. His father had purchased a small piece of land from a fellow villager, to build a makeshift house. He had paid Rs.10,000 in the beginning and promised to pay the remaining Rs.10,000 in small instalments, as and when he could accumulate money. He kept paying Rs. 500–1000 per month, but he was charged an interest of 5% per month. Surendra's father used to work from early in the morning to late at night. His father fell sick and subsequently passed away. His 10-year-old brother had to take up the responsibility of working like their father. Surendra also started working at his home. A local trafficker came to know about their vulnerable situation and approached their mother. He gave her false hope of better education for her kids, in return for light labour. His promises convinced her and she gave consent to the child trafficker to recruit her sons. When he tried to take them out of the village, the person who had sold them their piece of land came to know about it. He picked a fight with the trafficker and made him release the elder boy. Surendra was taken to

Jaipur. There was no communication between Surendra and his mother. Weeks turned into months. After six months, he was rescued from a factory during a police raid in February 2019.

During this time his family had been thrown out from the land that they partially owned. His mother and elder brother had shifted to the mother's village in a neighbouring district—Nawada.

5
Familial Trafficking

Radhika, 14, and her younger sister Vedika, 12, were handed over by their father, to their aunt who ran a music and dance troupe company. The company employed over 25 women, 14 of them below the age of 18. After months with the troupe, Radhika was helped by a young engineer to escape the troupe. She was produced before the Child Welfare Committee (CWC), Patna. The CWC after recording her statement ordered the Superintendent of Police to lodge an FIR and rescue the rest of the girls, including Radhika's younger sister. Subsequently, the Anti-Human Trafficking Unit (AHTU) of the district raided the premises of her aunt's company and rescued nine women, three of them were below the age of 18. They found that following Radhika's escape, her sister Vedika was beaten, tortured, and hacked to death by their aunt and her bouncers; they were torturing her to obtain information about the whereabouts of her elder sister Radhika, which she was completely unaware of.

At the premises, the AHTU seized used and unused condoms and libido-enhancing drugs. This led to the conclusion that commercial sexual exploitation was going on under the garb of music and dance performance.

The incident was a case of familial child trafficking for commercial sexual exploitation. This illegal activity is going on rampantly under the garb of music and dance troupes, in several districts across Bihar.

The major challenges which surface in familial trafficking are rehabilitation, securing justice for the sex trafficking survivors and prosecution of the offenders who are committing grave human rights violations. In this case, both girls had been sold off by their father who had separated from their mother, who had married another man.

Radhika had nothing to fall back on except institutional care, such as shelters that protect trafficking survivors. Who would file for her compensation? How would she fight her legal battle? What would happen to her after she turns 18? What are the support systems available for her to help start a life outside of the shelter home? Radhika is currently residing in an institutional care center run by the state and is picking up her studies. There are tens of thousands of sex trafficking survivors who face similar challenges. Such girls go through immense pain and trauma which stays with them for a long time or is lifelong in most cases.

Currently, there is a major vacuum in the rehabilitation scheme in the country. There is no legislation which talks about rehabilitation as the right of trafficking survivors. There is no clear mandate for transitioning the survivors to community-based support system or help for recovery.

A large number of girls engaged in orchestra groups in Bihar are facilitated by family members. There are cases where advances as high as two lakh rupees have been received by the parents of the young girls. This is provided ahead of the marriage season which is when there is demand for the dance and music troupe companies. The parents commit that their daughter will perform for the music and dance troupe company for the next 4-6 months. Strikingly, law enforcement agencies and anti-trafficking stakeholders overlook familial trafficking, which is when a family member or guardian is the survivor's trafficker or the one who sells the child to a third-party trafficker.

Familial trafficking is unique and difficult to identify because it takes place within family networks and victimizes children, mostly under the age of 12. These children often do not realise that they are victims. Because of this, the indicators for familial trafficking are different from the indicators for other types of trafficking. In these cases, the trafficker may begin grooming the victim at an early age, using their close proximity to take advantage of the child's developmental stage and inability to verbally express concerns or safety issues.

In these cases, the child's inherent loyalty to and reliance on the family structure make familial trafficking difficult to identify and challenging to prosecute. There are many misconceptions about familial traffickings, such as the belief that familial trafficking only occurs within neighbourhoods, communities, or countries of low socioeconomic status. This contributes to challenges in prosecution, prevention, and protection efforts.

Addressing familial trafficking requires an interdisciplinary approach to ensure: recovery of the mental and physical health of the victim, trauma-informed investigation and prosecutorial efforts, survivor-led and survivor-centered practices and interventions, and societal education and awareness. When the family member is the trafficker, the exploitation is often normalised and accepted within the family culture, and it sometimes spans generations. This normalisation of exploitation may also occur when familial trafficking is tied to economic and cultural factors, such as in cases of forced child labour in music and dance troupes.

If another family member notices the exploitation of the child, there is a strong incentive to look the other way to protect the family, both physically and in reputation, from outside interventions. Family members entrusted with caring for the children are often the ones grooming, manipulating, abusing, and exploiting them. In many of these cases, children may simply have no other dependable adults actively engaged in their lives. They also may not have the physical and mental development to identify coercive tactics being used by an individual they have bonded with, trust, and love. Because children are dependent on their families for their basic needs such as food, shelter, and clothing, they are often faced with having basic needs unmet or physical violence if they don't comply with the trafficker.

The traumatic impacts are severe because children have little psychological recourse for protecting themselves from the trafficker, who may also wield significant power by nature of the familial relationship alone. When the family member or guardian is the victim's trafficker, it may not be apparent that human trafficking is occurring, especially because the victim lives with or near the perpetrator. Whether the parent or guardian is the trafficker or sells the child who is then placed in the control of another trafficker, the trafficker is both the exploiter and caregiver.

A child in this situation is often trained not to report what is happening. In such a scenario, when the child interacts with adults who might otherwise notice a problem or identify the child as vulnerable, such as teachers, neighbours, doctors, and other adults in the community, they are perceived as shy or failing to thrive.

Furthermore, victims of familial trafficking might not be able to comprehend or identify with the indicators featured in most public awareness and outreach campaigns that share information on how to seek help. These campaigns typically target audiences who are much older than those exploited in familial trafficking.

The reality is that abuse, pain, torture, and exploitation are the only existence these survivors may have known. The impacts of familial trafficking, both visible and not, and subsequent needs of survivors are often severe and complex, and they can be exacerbated by the onset of trauma during key childhood developmental stages. When children experience familial trafficking, they may develop educational and social delays, physical health problems, and psychological disorders, such as complex post-traumatic stress disorder and attachment disorders. Survivors may encounter a large number of health indicators and somatic complaints due to having to endure trauma for a long period of time at an early age, including head, stomach, and body aches; throat and urinary tract infections; interrupted sleep due to nightmares and flashbacks; difficulty concentrating; asthma; and more.

Survivors of familial trafficking have a range of responses to the traditional educational system: some are reported to have learning challenges, including illiteracy and processing challenges. Other children excel, whether because school is where they feel safe or because they have been conditioned to please adults in their lives or developed resiliency and survival skills early in life. Furthermore, familial trafficking situations may have prevented survivors from developing key healthy social skills, including how to make and maintain friends, relate to other children and adults, ask for assistance, and recognize their own self-worth.

Having a family member as the main perpetrator and trafficker may also result in many victims feeling unable to speak about the experiences they endured due to the shame it may bring upon their families, communities, and themselves. Regardless of socioeconomic background, child survivors of familial trafficking situations often have limited avenues for seeking assistance. Frequently, service providers use the same approaches and resources for familial trafficking that are used for all types of human trafficking, which can be inappropriate and even harmful. Few resources have been developed to address the particularities of familial trafficking. The ways in which a service provider would engage with a ten-year-old child exploited by a family member will need to be different than when engaging with a child who has a safe home with a trusted adult. A child who has been exploited by a family member will most likely need services to address complex trauma, attachment, and severe exploitation. While awareness of familial trafficking is increasing, more research is needed.

Still, the specific and long-term needs of survivors of familial trafficking can be met in a variety of ways. For example, many children would benefit from having one-on-one support to develop an individualized program with the survivor and meet with them several times a week. Most importantly, age-and culture-appropriate comprehensive programs need to be developed with consideration of each unique survivor in mind. Positive connection, the freedom to experience developmentally appropriate activities, and even fun, sometimes for the first time, are healing elements that should be emphasized in these programs. Through programs with an increased focus on familial trafficking, survivors learn they are not alone in their journey and that someone is there to walk beside them through every step.

6

Can Prosecution Prevent Child Trafficking?

At the time of the 2011 census, India was home to around 10.13 million child labourers between the ages of 5–14 years. Despite being illegal, child trafficking, and bonded labour are widespread. Child labour persists, often with impunity for child traffickers and limited legal recourse for survivors. The common denominator for survivors is vulnerability: they are insecure and at risk, they don't know their rights, and even if they come to know with the help of others, they are unable to obtain justice.

Section 370 of the Indian Penal Code (IPC) has criminalised trafficking offenses that involve exploitation—any act of physical exploitation or any form of sexual exploitation, slavery, or practices similar to slavery, and servitude. Section 370 prescribes penalties ranging from seven to 10 years imprisonment and a fine for offenses involving an adult victim, and 10 years to life imprisonment and a fine for those involving a child victim. These penalties are sufficiently stringent and, with respect to sex trafficking, commensurate with those prescribed for other serious crimes, such as kidnapping. However, Section 370 is not used consistently across trafficking cases. Police continue to file trafficking cases under the Juvenile Justice Act, Child Labour Act and other sections of the IPC, which criminalise traffickers and oppressive employers who force children to work; however, these provisions are unevenly enforced, and some of their prescribed penalties are not sufficiently stringent, mandating only fines or short prison sentences.

According to the National Crime and Records Bureau (NCRB) 2019 Report, a total of 2,088 trafficking cases were reported under the IPC compared to 1,830 trafficking cases in 2018 and 2,854 trafficking cases reported in 2017. In 2019, out of 600 prosecutions completed, 306 traffickers were convicted in 160 cases, and 1,329 suspects were acquitted in 440 cases. The acquittal rate for trafficking cases was close to 73 percent in 2019. In 2018, the prosecution completed 545 cases, convicting 322 traffickers in 95 cases, and acquitting 1,124 suspects in 450 cases, with 83 percent of cases resulting in acquittal.

Following the nationwide lockdown, regular court proceedings and evidence collection were suspended. The Supreme Court of India encouraged courts across the country to utilise online technologies to continue hearing trafficking cases virtually during the pandemic. There have been cases in Gaya district when the accused threatened the prosecution witnesses (rescued child) and their family with dire consequences if they did not turn hostile in the court while recording their testimonies. There are cases where the accused tried abducting the witnesses, but except in one case, no FIR was ever registered against the accused by the police for intimidating the witnesses. In December 2020, the Supreme Court directed the states, including Bihar, to ensure that video conferencing facilities were available for children and trafficking witnesses to help mitigate case delays and to save the time and cost incurred by the witnesses who otherwise had to travel to courts.

The survivors often require legal assistance from charity organisations and independent lawyers. This assistance is wide-ranging: ensuring that strong FIRs, with all relevant sections, are registered by the police; briefing the public prosecutor; pursuing other remedies for survivors, such as providing them protection, with the support of police, against intimidation and threats from the accused. Child trafficking cases often span out over more than two states. The trafficked children are rescued from various states and returned to their native place. Their summons is never served on time, and this allows them very little time to travel to another state where the matter is listed. In some cases, the traffickers and the police together visit the homes of the rescued children to serve the summons.

After the rescue, a criminal case is lodged. Often the subsequent police investigation and prosecution result in the conviction of the accused only if the victim is supported by any charity organisations. They work very closely with the survivor and help with: lodging an FIR; charging the accused with specific sections of human trafficking laws; support in accessing their compensation; legal assistance, which includes transporting the witness to the court where the matter is listed, to helping them obtain justice.

There is a huge gap in collaboration even between charity organisations. Charity organisations rarely request advice and assistance from each other, for reasons unknown to me. Collaboration between NGOs that have acquired legal experience, skills and know-how in pursuing cases would help increase prosecution rates and improve legal outcomes for the survivors. However, there are only a limited number of charity organisations assisting with prosecutions.

Collaboration is particularly important in inter-state cases where charity organisations cannot always undertake investigations in neighbouring states where the children are rescued from factories. Given the large distances involved, charities in the state where the child is rescued are also unable to protect and prepare the survivors for trial once they return to their home state.

For example, in cases where the rescue and trial occur outside the home state of the survivor, the survivors are eventually reintegrated with their home state. In such a scenario, a charity organisation in their home state could take over the process of rehabilitation and witness protection.

The survivors are often harassed, intimidated, and vulnerable to social stigma. On top of poor investigations for many reasons, slow trials and child unfriendly court environments result in the victim feeling further victimised. While charity organisations and private lawyers do not replace the police or public prosecutors, they can support and assist survivors at every step of the process, ensuring greater accountability and better outcome. This support improves the survivor's experience of the criminal justice system, and is highly likely to improve the chance of a conviction as in Ashish's case.

Recording Testimonies Via Video

The Supreme Court had been contemplating the question of allowing online testimony in cases of inter-state child trafficking. The court had asked all states and union territories to submit the number of cases that required children to appear in other states for recording their testimonies. This move would change the course of history in the realm of prosecution and increase the rate of convictions in child trafficking cases. It would bring great succour in the lives of child trafficking survivors and reduce the incidences of child trafficking.

Socially and economically marginalised communities in India are most vulnerable to the trap of child trafficking. This includes those officially categorised as scheduled castes, members of tribal communities and religious minorities. Despite various initiatives by the government for affirmative action, there is rampant poverty and illiteracy among these communities as compared to the general population. Additionally, they often lack viable livelihood opportunities and financial services, resulting in a vicious cycle of poverty. Laws exist to protect these communities; however, enforcement remains weak. These workers often migrate from poor rural areas where they cannot earn decent wages and are susceptible to exploitation. Despite the existence of strong anti-trafficking laws, these are rarely enforced and workers often do not have fair terms of employment, health insurance or access to other entitlements. Discrimination and differences in language and culture can compound these problems.

There is no denying the fact that prosecution alone will not bring an end to child trafficking, but legal strategies have immense potential to deliver justice to survivors, deter potential perpetrators and put traffickers out of an easy-money business.

As per the Witness Protection Scheme, 2018, police protection should be provided to survivors whose FIR is registered in the same police district. However, in cases of child trafficking survivors, the FIRs are registered in the places where they are rescued from rather than their home district. These children face a lot of procedural and technical challenges upon coming back to their native state. They face threats of re-trafficking and they also fear testifying against their traffickers.

The child trafficking survivors rescued in another state do not get protection under the witness protection scheme upon returning home, despite facing constant threats from the traffickers.

Another challenge they face in accessing compensation under the victim compensation scheme. They cannot claim this from the District Legal Services Authority of their home districts since their legal case is usually filed outside their native state upon rescue.

Once the survivors are reunited with their families through the procedures laid down in the Juvenile Justice Act, 2015, most survivors have to fight their own battle. The official outreach and protection services hardly ever reach them. Back home with their family and community, they face multiple challenges. First, they face a strong threat of re-trafficking by the same child trafficker. Second, they face constant threats and intimidation not to go to court even if they are called to testify against their trafficker. Third, how to have two square meals? Fourth, there is no support for their holistic rehabilitation.

But now there is a silver lining in the realm of prosecution of inter-state child trafficking cases as the Supreme Court of India has ordered to carry out the testifying process via video-conferencing. It chose two cases to begin with: a case between the Jaipur POCSO Court and the Gaya POCSO Court, and the other was between the Sitamarhi POCSO Court and Additional District Judge and Sessions Court, Karkardooma, Delhi. These two cases were picked up by the Supreme Court on a pilot basis to see how justice for the child trafficking survivors can be made available at their doorstep with the adaptation of digital technologies in the justice system.

Both cases showed a tremendous amount of coordination and cooperation between the states and among various functionaries within the state to make sure that the child trafficking survivors get justice.

In the Gaya case, there were a total of eight witnesses; four child trafficking survivors and a guardian each. They were from the Manjhi community. The dates were scheduled for the first week of March, 2021. All summons were served to their addresses by the District Legal Services Authority. Four of them received it, and the rest were not available at their addresses, but the summons were posted on the door of their houses. .

On the given dates, only six of them turned up. As they entered the court, two people walked up to them and told them to tell the judge that the children had gone to study not work. The District Legal Services Authority was coordinating the whole process. Sharp at 10 am, a retired judge who was appointed as a Remote Point Coordinator arrived at the POCSO court, with the necessary papers. All three children were sitting on a couch looking around at the walls of the court which was full of paintings. Since it was child-friendly court there were stories books too. The children in the court appeared relaxed and calm. They were also whispering and smiling. There was also a support person appointed by the Child Welfare Committee on the request of the District Legal Services Authority, who helped the children to settle down.

The support person enquired why two of the witnesses, a child and his mother, did not come. They said that the father of the child was in a hospital in Aligarh, Uttar Pradesh, he had developed COVID like symptoms, and the mother and child were taking care of him at the hospital.

Technical assistants were busy checking the internet connectivity with the Jaipur court. Soon the process began. On the first day, all three children testified and were cross-examined by the defence lawyer. All children, one by one, said that they were made to work right from 6 am to 9 pm every day, with a lunch break at 2 pm. How were they brought to Jaipur from Gaya? The defence lawyer was smart enough to ask questions in such a way that the children without realising what they were saying were largely rebutting what they had said at the beginning. Both the support person and the Remote Point Coordinator had to help the children understand the questions well so that they could answer them. The two accused were present in the Jaipur court, and they were shown to the children through the video. The children recognised the perpetrators sitting among many others. There was good network connectivity throughout the process.

The day-one process was over. Three children and their fathers went out of the court talking about the process, questions, and wondering about the science and technology that made the online court possible.

On the second day, all the three parents arrived at the POCSO court premises well on time. The process got started with recording their testimonies. One of the fathers told the court during the process that his 11 years old child was still with the accused working in his bangle-making factory in Jaipur. "All children were rescued from the accused's factory in the month of February, 2019. Even after many requests, my child was not freed. When I went to Jaipur to bring the child back after my first child was rescued, they did allow me to bring my child. I could not even see my child in Jaipur. I had been under tremendous pressure since then to turn hostile in the court," the father said. Just after the process was over, and it was revealed that his younger son was still in the clutches of the trafficker, he was taken to the Superintendent of Police, Gaya, who asked them to go to the police station that was situated in his village. The next day, he submitted a written complaint with the Station House Officer. The child was released and sent back home after a few days.

The next date for hearing for the remaining two witnesses—a child and his mother—was fixed just after Holi in April.

The District Legal Services Authority again tried to serve the summons to the remaining witness, but they could not, as the family was not in Gaya. They were working at a brick kiln in Aligarh, Uttar Pradesh. Many families migrate in search of employment during the lean agriculture season. This family was one among them. The Support Person managed to get their current address and contact numbers. He contacted them and told them about the date for the hearing that was fixed only for them. If they did not come and participate in the process, the summons would convert into a non-bailable warrant next time. The mother requested the Support Person

Can Prosecution Prevent Child Trafficking? | 107

to talk with the owner of the brick kiln. On reaching out, the owner said that he had got around 50 families from Bihar to work in his brick kiln. "I have nothing to do with them; everything was decided by the contractor who brought the families here, so you please speak with the contractor". This contractor was a human trafficker dealing with families, and when he was contacted, he refused to send them to Gaya for the court process. He said that earlier he was approached by Asadullah and Sherjahan— the accused in the case—to allow the mother and son to go to speak in favour of the accused, but he did not allow them to go because he had paid Rs. 40,000 in advance, so they had to work until the advance was settled. The family was trapped in another human trafficking racket in Uttar Pradesh, which was run by a local trafficker from Gaya who would send hundreds of families across many states to work in coercive conditions. Such families are in high demand in Uttar Pradesh, Haryana and Punjab to work in brick kilns and farms. The human trafficker did not show any fear for law, or subsequent prosecution while denying them a leave to participate in the court process in Gaya.

The online court process did not happen at the scheduled date. Later two dates were fixed for hearing by the designated court in Jaipur, to no avail. The pilot case in the country was getting delayed just because of a human trafficker who was effectively holding the witnesses as hostage. This was happening while the country was being gripped by the second deadly wave of COVID-19. The family came back home in the last week of June. The fourth date for hearing was fixed for the last week of July. The summons was served to them at their home in Barmoria, a village that was around 50 km away from the district headquarters. The family received the summons for the first time and worried about its consequences, and consulted many in the village. Everyone suggested they go to court and speak about what had happened to their child. The mother-son duo arrived in Gaya, a day in advance, and went to the court to participate in the process well before the scheduled time. They reached the Gaya POCSO Court.. They were received warmly by the district legal services staff and offered a cushioned couch to sit on. They were looking all around, and the sight of the court was eye-soothing. They felt a bit relaxed, but still worried about the process. Everything was in order. The designated judge to assist as remote point coordinator was interacting with the witnesses, making them comfortable as he sensed both of them were worried. The link for the video conference arrived from the Jaipur court. The technical person connected both the courts online. The Jaipur judge sat in his chair to start the process. But the court was told that the defence lawyer was not present, so the next date for hearing was fixed for the first week of August. The development was shared with the mother and son who were aghast over the development. They said to the support person, "we had to spend Rs. 1200 to come over here, stay in a hotel, incur expenditures on travel and food, and lost two days' wages. Do we have to come again?" They were told about the new date for the hearing. They went back home. On the scheduled date, they arrived in court. And asked about the defence lawyer's presence in the court from the support person. He asked them to wait. The online court process started sharp at 11 am. The defence lawyer was once again not present in the court. The presiding judge in the Jaipur Court took it seriously and ordered to cancel the bail of the two accused for child trafficking. They were on bail and had been out in the open for months. The accused surrendered in the court after having played hide-and-seek with police for a week, and they moved applications for their bail. They got bail the next day. Now, the matter was again listed for recording of testimonies. The designated courts—Jaipur and Gaya District Legal Services Authority—were busy executing all necessary procedures to make sure that everything would fall in place. However, the mother-son duo did not appear for the hearing and their whereabouts were not known.

The next date for the same was set in September, but they did not turn up. It was scheduled again for the first week of October 2021. They did not turn up this time too. But surprisingly the elder brother of the rescued child was produced in the court by the Gaya Police, though he was not allowed to testify by the court. While the mother and son were present in the Jaipur Court for recording their testimonies. The designated judge recorded their testimonies, but they reportedly turned hostile. The child trafficking survivor's version was that he was brought to Jaipur by the accused for education in a convent school, and his mother too reportedly recorded the same version.

While writing about the developments in the case, I am wondering how the Supreme Court's order was flouted in this case, since the order which designated the case to be heard online was not fully complied with. Out of eight witnesses, the six went online and the remaining two finally appeared in the Jaipur court clearly under the control of the child traffickers. It shows how the traffickers can use their power to influence justice. The child trafficking survivors can only obtain justice as long as they are protected under the Witness Protection Scheme, 2018, and supported very closely, even with travel expenses, by the District Legal Services Authority. If no special arrangements are made for them, the child traffickers will relentlessly keep exploiting the children of the under-privileged sections.

After the successful completion of the two pilot cases, the Supreme Court of India in the first week of February 2022 has issued an standard operating procedure directing to record statements/evidence of child witnesses/victims of human trafficking cases via video-conferencing from a government facility within the local jurisdiction of the residence of such children.

7

Most of the Child Labourers Are Musahars

During the course of writing this book, I met close to 350 child labourers. Out of which 276 were Musahars. Majority of them live in tiny huts in villages, although their cluster of huts is situated far away from the main village population. Their mud houses are generally without doors and windows.

They are a community with many progressive ideas. In the Musahar community, women enjoy almost equal status with men. Musahar women in general are not confined to the four walls of the house. In fact, it is women who run homes, although wife-beating does take place very frequently. The women make decisions about purchasing household items, finalising marriage proposals, deciding who to approach when someone in the family is sick, etc. Men give almost all their daily wage earning to their wives and keep some aside for liquor. They do not have any preference for sons. For them both girls and boys are equal. Sharing and caring among Musahars is very common. Many a time the children of one family are fed by another family.

The Musahars are very honest and loyal. They are not assertive and aggressive in normal circumstances, even in their fight for rights.

Musahars are largely agricultural labourers. Both men and women work as labourers to earn as much as they can to keep the wolf from the door. The major expense for a Musahar family is food. Whenever work is available, both men and women work as daily wage labourers to earn as much as they can. For most families, the daily wages barely get them through the day. They spend a major chunk of their earnings on food every day. When they do not get any work, and if they have not migrated to other states, they sell the grain they earned as wages during the harvesting season to manage their expenses.

After food, the highest percentage of expense is incurred in medical care. They spend very little on clothing. The majority of them do not possess even a small piece of land for cultivation. Due to the efforts of charity organisations or other government drives, a few of the households have bank accounts but with little or no money deposited in the accounts. Business and other self-employment ventures are rare.

Expenses such as marriage, sickness and funerals, which don't spare any of the households, whenever they occur, washes away their savings. These circumstances also force them to borrow money from the local money lenders, at an exorbitantly high rate of interest—nearly 5 percent per month, which becomes a whopping 60 percent per annum. They fall into the debt trap and seldom come out of it. In some cases, the debt continues to the next generation.

Consumption of liquor is rampant among them, even a good number of women also drink. There are some men who drink throughout the day. This drinking habit eats away their hard-earned savings. They remain poor.

Their children are also very hardworking, hardy and honest. Illiteracy, landlessness, complete lack of local employment, and debt-incurring expenses make them quite vulnerable to the machinations of trafficking.

Gaya: A Hotbed of Child Trafficking

Gaya tops the list in terms of the numbers of child labourers. As per the census held in 2011, Bihar has 10,88,509 child labourers of which 78,929 are from Gaya.

Children are trafficked to destinations outside the state by local traffickers, but the most favoured destination for them is bangle factories in Jaipur, Rajasthan. According to the Child Welfare Committee, since 2014 a total of 1,200 child trafficking survivors have returned to the district; they were rescued from other states like Delhi, Andhra Pradesh, Maharashtra, Himachal Pradesh and Rajasthan.

There are 13 districts in Bihar which are highly affected by the issue of child trafficking, but Gaya tops the list.

The number of rescued children is just the tip of the iceberg. Almost all rescue operations were carried out with the active participation of NGOs.

A three-pronged strategy of prevention, protection and prosecution have been devised to fight the crime, but prosecution gets the least attention of stakeholders. I strongly feel that without prosecuting the local traffickers, fighting child trafficking becomes extremely difficult.

The Department of Labour Resources, Bihar, developed a state action plan to combat child labour in 2009, which was later amended as The State Action Plan for Elimination of Child Labour, Prohibition and Regulation of Adolescent Labour, 2017. The State Action plan was drafted meticulously, it has many provisions right from the state level to the panchayat level. It details formation of committees, which would bring together 14 departments to carry out their mandated activities in preventing, rescuing, prosecuting and rehabilitating the rescued child labourers. It was sweeping in recommendations. The action plan has been waiting to come into effect years after it has been passed. Since then, there have been two national lockdowns and an unprecedented reverse migration of child labourers. A large number of children came back from their workplaces, some alone and some with their families. Most of them were re-trafficked after the lockdown was lifted.

8

Efficiency of Anti-Human Trafficking Units in the Country

In 2006, the Central Government of India, through the Ministry of Home Affairs, in partnership with the United Nations Office on Drugs and Crime took up a project for 'Strengthening the law enforcement response in India against trafficking in persons through training and capacity building'. This was aimed at raising awareness among law enforcement officers (police and prosecutors) about the problem of human trafficking and to build their capacity to better investigate and prosecute human traffickers perpetrating the crime.

One of the objectives of the project was the establishment of Anti Human Trafficking Units (AHTUs) at the district level in five states: Bihar, Maharashtra, West Bengal, Goa, and Andhra Pradesh. These states were selected as they represent source, destination and transit areas for human trafficking of different types, including trafficking of women and children for commercial sexual exploitation, child labour, forced labour, bonded labour and others.

In 2010, the Central Government through the Ministry of Home Affairs issued an advisory notification with the subject 'Comprehensive Scheme for Establishment of integrated Anti Human Trafficking Units and capacity building of responders, including Training of Trainers for strengthening the law enforcement response to human trafficking in India Plan.' It directed the state governments across the country to notify AHTUs in their districts to be responsible for the registration of complaints and investigation of all cases related to human trafficking.

The advisory notification specified that AHTUs would address all three aspects of trafficking, namely prevention, protection and prosecution. Further, the AHTUs would be responsible for developing databases on traffickers and networking with all other concerned agencies.

The state governments were mandated to set up AHTUs at the district headquarters level, with funds provided under the scheme for infrastructure and development. The state governments would also be responsible to provide police personnel and officials from other departments to manage the AHTU. The police officials would directly report to the Superintendent of Police of their respective districts.

A national-level study—A national study on the status of anti-human trafficking units in India (2010-2019)—was done to measure the efficacy of the AHTUs set up to fight against human trafficking. It was carried out by a Kolkata-based organisation—SANJOG—the winner of the prestigious Stop Slavery Award-2021. The study brought out startling facts. It found that if a trafficking survivor or their family member goes to file a complaint at their local police station, more often than not the investigation is done by the local police and there is no straightforward way for the complaint to be investigated by the jurisdictional AHTU without approaching a court of law to make a special request for the same.

One sex trafficking survivor shared her negative experience with the local police, stating that they unnecessarily delayed recording her statement under Section 164 of CrPC, were rude to her and only agreed to record the statement after intervention by a local NGO. The investigating officer had intimidated her by repeatedly telling her that it "would be better" if she stayed in a shelter home, despite her assertion that she had a supportive family with whom she lived. With legal assistance, a protest petition was filed before the local court, which ordered reinvestigation and transfer of the case to AHTU.

Another survivor spoke about her family's experience with the local police in West Bengal. She had been trafficked. Her parents had filed an FIR with the local police. When the survivor found out that she had been trafficked to Gujarat, she was able to call her parents who intimated the police about her location. Even though the police were cooperative with her father, who had filed the FIR, the police had no money or resources to travel to Gujarat. A few months later, she was trafficked back to West Bengal (South 24 Parganas district) and was able to inform her family, who helped the police with the rescue. However, even for this rescue within West Bengal, her father had to bear all the travel costs, as the police claimed to have no resources at all. Therefore, it is seen that the local police experience significant resource constraints, which can adversely affect their reach and ability to perform investigations and rescue operations.

With respect to the functioning of AHTUs, NGOs stated that AHTUs were functional, if not very active in Bihar, Tamil Nadu and Andhra Pradesh (whose AHTUs act as part of the Criminal Investigation Department). In Jharkhand and New Delhi, AHTUs were reported as very active (they are functional in eight districts in Jharkhand) and sometimes worked with NGOs on trafficking cases.

It was seen that registering trafficking cases with relevant sections from different laws was very challenging, as the police would resist the more detailed investigation that would inevitably be required. AHTU officials and local police were said to be reluctant to respond and act in trafficking cases, preferring instead to work on 'clearer' cases (theft, assault, etc.). They often prioritised other duties over their AHTU duties. The problem of survivors turning hostile, local traffickers getting out on bail or never getting arrested, and principal traffickers not being tracked down by AHTUs were some of the common problems faced by survivors in all states. When NGOs got involved in investigations, like inter-state investigations, AHTU officials would get pressured and claim to feel overworked. This clearly shows that the AHTUs are not sufficiently trained and there needs to be a Standard Operating Procedure (SOP) in place, governing responses and procedures for AHTUs. New Delhi's AHTUs are seen to have low caseloads, in spite of reports of human trafficking around Delhi, with the exact cause requiring further research. However, the functioning of AHTUs in New Delhi was found to be efficient; cases registered under them were well investigated. In Maharashtra, AHTUs only deal with pre-rescue investigation and rescue of survivors, after which the cases are transferred to local police stations that do not have the resources or training to carry out investigations properly, leading to unsuccessful prosecutions.

In Bihar and Tamil Nadu, the lack of coordination between law enforcement and other agencies has been said to have adversely impacted the entire system. Inter-departmental work that coordinates rescue, social welfare, compensation and other needs of survivors are extremely weak and NGOs in several states opined that there was no state interest in trafficking whatsoever. Due to these reasons, an SOP has not been developed for the AHTUs in Bihar, and there is no proper state policy on human trafficking for Tamil Nadu. AHTUs have stayed a low priority after the division of Andhra Pradesh and Telangana, while Jharkhand's large tribal population and their marginalisation have resulted in their voices not being heard—tribal migration and trafficking are not a high enough priority for the state.

In Maharashtra the disconnect between AHTUs and the local police harms investigation of cases and rescue operations. According to a Delhi-based NGO carrying out activities in Uttar Pradesh and Manipur, AHTUs are unable to fulfil their mandates due to the inaction of state and UT governments that hold the responsibility of setting up and facilitating the AHTUs.

9

Survivors Hardly Get Their Compensations

Section 357-A of the Code of Criminal Procedure, 1973, mandates that every state government, in coordination with the central government, shall prepare a scheme to provide funds to compensate human trafficking victims or their dependents, among others, who have suffered loss or injury as a result of the crime and who require rehabilitation. The Code of Criminal Procedure further provides for an indicative procedure to provide compensation, designating responsibilities to the jurisdictional District Legal Services Authority (DLSA) through the criminal injury compensation board or State Legal Services Authority (SLSA) to decide the quantum of compensation payable in different cases. The provision also contemplates trial courts making recommendations for compensation in certain cases.

At this time, about 25 states and seven UTs have implemented victim compensation schemes for various crimes, including rehabilitation for human trafficking, or loss or injury caused due to human trafficking. Every scheme has a schedule, containing particulars of compensation for various crimes, often prescribing maximum limits of compensation payable for different crimes.

In 2017, SANJOG had analysed victim compensation schemes of 13 States and filed RTIs in five states to gather data on implementation of Victim Compensation (VC) schemes and budget utilisation. Some of the observations made were: there is no uniformity in compensation amounts mandated by various states, the number of VC applications filed and the number of victims who received compensation was very low, there was a lack of awareness about the schemes and the application process itself was not victim-centric.

The results of the inquiry provided an overall picture of how victim compensation schemes are being implemented. For clarity, the findings are divided to reflect the process: from funds sanctioned to final receipt of compensation by victims. The data from 30 states and UTs have been compiled for this report, while two states did not respond to their RTI applications. The action research, through case studies and lived experiences, has provided a microanalysis of the systemic challenges faced by survivors applying for and receiving victim compensation. Through this action research, the organisation was able to assess service delivery by different actors in the system and was able to understand systemic responses towards the overall rehabilitation process.

Some states did not provide data, and other states provided false or discrepant data, and have been flagged. The data provided in the table below indicates the overall funds sanctioned and utilized for victim compensation schemes in the States/UTs. No specific data breakdown was provided for funds sanctioned exclusively for human trafficking. The data provided is from the year of institution of the victim compensation scheme till date. **The full report is available in the appendix.**

10
Silver Lining For Survivors: Draft of Anti-Trafficking Bill-2021

A draft of the anti-human trafficking bill had been passed in the Lok Sabha in 2018 but was never introduced in Rajya Sabha.

The objective of the bill is: To prevent and counter human trafficking, especially of women and children; to provide care, protection, and rehabilitation to the victims, while respecting their rights; create a supportive legal, economic and social environment for victims; and ensure prosecution of offenders.

While the 2018 bill dealt with trafficking, rescue, protection and rehabilitation of victims, the 2021 bill expands the scope to also include offences taking place outside India. The new bill also makes the National Investigation Agency (NIA) the central investigation authority looking into such offences.

What the Bill Says

According to the draft bill, the law applies to citizens of India, residing within and outside the country; persons on any ship or aircraft registered in India; foreign nationals and stateless people who have residency in India.

It also says the law "shall apply to every offence of trafficking in persons with cross-border implications."

The draft bill also widens the definition of the "victim" by including transgenders, besides women and children.

Once the bill becomes an act, the central government will notify and set up a National Anti-Trafficking Committee, while state governments will set up committees at state and district levels to ensure effective implementation.

The Bill proposes that any offence of trafficking "shall be punished with rigorous imprisonment for a term which shall not be less than seven years but which may extend to ten years, and shall also be liable to fine which shall not be less than one lakh rupees".

In addition, similar to the 2018-version, the new draft proposes more severe penalties for 'aggravated offences' and seeks to crackdown on organised crime syndicates. Aggravated offences include cases that may result in the death of the victim or where the victim suffers a grievous injury (in cases such as an acid attack), organ mutilation or removal of organs, or where the victim is a child.

According to the provisions of the draft: 'Whoever commits the offence of aggravated form of trafficking of a person shall be punishable with rigorous imprisonment for a term for ten years, but which may extend to imprisonment for life and shall also be liable to fine which may extend to ten lakh rupees.'

In case of the death of the victim, the bill proposes life imprisonment along with a fine of Rs. 30 lakhs. The bill also proposes imprisonment of up to 20 years and death penalty for the offenders found guilty. 'The person shall be punished with rigorous imprisonment for twenty years, but which may extend to life, or in case of second or subsequent conviction with death, and with fine which may extend up to thirty lakh rupees.'

The bill also says that the investigation needs to be completed within 90 days from the date of the arrest of the accused. The Bill widens the range of offenders who can be booked under the law, bringing public servants, armed forces personnel, or anyone in a position of authority under its ambit. Penalty for the guilty will include life imprisonment along with a fine of Rs. 30 lakhs.

However, there are activists, lawyers and civil society organisations fighting against human trafficking who think that the draft bill is not up to the mark and that it misses out on many important features that should have been included. Hence they have been engaged in advocacy with the central government to accommodate the missed-out features.

They say that handing over the investigation in trafficking crimes to the NIA would not be optimal. Some believe that it would burden the already overstretched unit further, and others argue that this move would be an attack on federalism since it removes local enforcement agencies from the picture. Reporting of offences has been made mandatory, with penalties for non-reporting, but those with an understanding of the tortuous processes, point to the fact that victims often do not want a complaint to be recorded. The mention of the death penalty for various forms of aggravated trafficking offences needs to be flagged too.

The Bill is silent over the rehabilitation fund, it does not specify a dedicated rehabilitation fund. A dedicated fund must be maintained for relief, rehabilitation, victim compensation, and funds for inter-and intra-state investigations. Without these allocated funds, the institutions will not be able to carry out their responsibilities in a timely and efficient manner.

Although the Bill enables greater choice for the rescued individual in choosing whether they want to stay at a shelter home or not, the rehabilitation is still mostly limited to shelter homes. Currently, there is no clear provision for reintegration and community-based rehabilitation. Community-based rehabilitation, a model that provides health services, legal aid, access to welfare schemes and income opportunities, is crucial for ensuring the reintegration of victims back into their community and family. The risk of re-trafficking is high unless the victims are provided economic support. The inclusion of job training and skill development in the rehabilitation process will empower victims to be financially independent and provide them with freedom and choice. This is particularly imperative in the pandemic and post-pandemic context.

In addition, the bill must provide greater agency to survivors to choose the duration of stay at shelter homes. This is necessary to provide them with the freedom to leave the institution if there is any exploitation or abuse, which is commonly reported. Equally important is to have checks and balances in place to ensure that shelter homes are safe places for survivors.

AHTU is a central institution in the current anti-human trafficking ecosystem. They have been responsible for the timely investigation of trafficking cases and for ensuring care and dignity for victims. However, the Bill does not mention AHTUs except once, thus failing to both clarify their role as well as to strengthen their functioning. Though various states have set up AHTUs, there is no uniformity across the country that will make it mandatory for AHTUs to investigate human trafficking cases. Therefore, a law that would set out the procedures and clarify what issue will be taken up by which body, is essential. Assigning this responsibility and accountability to a dedicated agency will ensure speedy investigation and aid for survivors.

Despite all these, the intention behind the bill is anything but laudable. However, it would be wise to review it to iron out the anomalies before it is passed.

Appendix

A. Victim Compensation Schemes: Analysis for 12 states

Abstract

This paper aims to analyse the procedural aspects of Victim Compensation Schemes (VCS) across 12 states, namely, Andhra Pradesh, Assam, Bihar, Chhattisgarh, Delhi, Jharkhand, Madhya Pradesh, Odisha, Rajasthan, Tamil Nadu, Uttar Pradesh, and West Bengal. The objective of the analysis is to highlight the differences in how these states have defined the objective of the scheme, " the victim", nodal and implementing agencies (including functions), funding sources for the scheme, eligibility criteria for the compensation, procedure, and amount of compensation being provided for human trafficking categories. Additionally, the state-wise performance of victim compensation schemes has been analysed by providing insights on the registration of cases, decision and pendency rate related to victim compensation at the Legal Service Authorities. Additionally, the allocation and usage of the Central Victim Compensation Fund across states have also been highlighted in this paper.

Introduction

Victim compensation is an integral part of the rehabilitation of victims of violence, trafficking and other related crimes. The 2009 amendment to the Code of Criminal Procedure (Section 357A) necessitates that state governments in coordination with the central government shall formulate schemes that will provide the necessary compensation to victims and their dependents. As per CPC, District Legal Service Authorities (DLSA) and State Legal Service Authorities (SLSA) have been made responsible for deciding the amount of compensation payable for different crimes. In accordance with the same, the 2018 National Legal Service Authority (NALSA) scheme for women victims/survivors of sexual assault/other crimes was developed, and state governments were directed to pay compensation in accordance with the scheme. Along with this scheme, several states have existing victim compensation schemes for other crimes (which are not a part of the NALSA scheme), with compensation amounts and procedures varying amongst states.

The analysis of the victim compensation schemes across states highlights the wide variance in procedures, categories for which survivors can apply for compensation, as well as the compensation amounts prescribed to different offences. Furthermore, even though the central government has issued a model scheme, several states are yet to revise their existing victim compensation schemes leading to disparities. The objective of this paper is to analyse the legal provisions of the victim compensation scheme in 12 states to highlight the discrepancies in procedural aspects. Additionally, the data analysis of the functioning of Legal Service Authorities and utilization of Central Victim Compensation Fund has also been added to provide insights on the functioning of the VC schemes across states.

Analysis of Victim Compensation Schemes

In this part, we will review the victim compensation schemes of 12 states in India. For comparison, the victim compensation schemes as notified by each state have been examined thoroughly. The schemes have been critically analysed on a set of parameters and a comparison has been made among the states. Of the total 36 States and UTs, 12 states—Andhra Pradesh, Assam, Bihar, Chhattisgarh, Delhi, Jharkhand, Madhya Pradesh, Odisha, Rajasthan, Tamil Nadu, Uttar Pradesh, and West Bengal—have been selected for the analysis. Each state has its own victim compensation scheme.

1. **Aims and Objectives of the Schemes**

    Most of the states had put forth similar objectives for the scheme as per section 357A of CrPc which provides a mandate for the constitution of the VCS:

A scheme to grant compensation to the victims or their dependents who sustain damage or hurt due to offenses and who require rehabilitation.

However, some states, notably, Madhya Pradesh, have attempted to make the scheme more inclusive. The MP state VCS provides for union and state government coordination for providing funds for compensation and deciding the quantum of compensation for the crime victims or dependents, according to their financial status, who have suffered loss or injury as a result of the crime and require rehabilitation

Odisha has also attempted to expand the scope of the scheme by including the following provisions:

a. Provides financial assistance to the victim

b. Support services such as shelter, counselling, medical aid, legal assistance, education, and vocational training depending on the needs of the victim.

2. Definition of Victims

The term "Victims" has been defined to include:

Any individual, who has suffered any loss or injury caused because of the criminal act or omission on the part of the accused and requires rehabilitation under this scheme and includes the guardian or legal heir of such person but does not include a person who is responsible for injury to such person.

Includes victim who is sexually exploited for commercial purposes, trafficking, a victim of acid attack, and also a dependent who is leading life on the income of the victim and who require rehabilitation.

The definition of the victim under the schemes largely follows the definition provided in CrPc, 1973.

Moreover, Section 357A of the criminal code intended to assist those victims as well for whom the case could not proceed for want of identification of the accused. Hence, the definition of victim somewhat does not seem to be in line with the scope of the scheme.

Interestingly, none of the state VC schemes define the term "rehabilitation". The discretion to define rehabilitation has been left with the state and district legal authorities to be decided on a case-by-case basis. This in our view is the biggest drawback of the scheme. Beneficiaries of rehabilitation, and what is included in such rehabilitation should have been defined clearly. A thorough analysis of the existing literature reveals that by logical inference, rehabilitation can include immediate medical support, emotional counselling, provisional accommodation, employment and skill training, and any financial assistance.

3. Nodal and Implementing Authority

Most states have delegated the tasks related to compensation and relief to the DLSA and SLSA. The nodal agency to oversee the implementation of the scheme is entrusted with various departments, including, home department, law department, excise department, etc. The table below shows state-wise nodal and implementing authorities.

Andhra Pradesh	State Home Department
Assam	Principal Secretary, State, Home Department
Bihar	State Law Department
Chhattisgarh	State Home Department
Delhi	SLSA
Jharkhand	Director, Prosecution, Government of Jharkhand
Madhya Pradesh	State Home Department
Odisha	SLSA
Rajasthan	SLSA
Tamil Nadu	Home, Prohibition and Excise Department

| Implementation authority | 1. All states have entrusted the task of deciding compensation and providing other interim reliefs to the DLSA/SLSA.
2. Few Exceptions being, Chhattisgarh & Jharkhand, where the task is entrusted with District Collector and District Magistrate, respectively. |
|---|---|

4. Financial Authority.

| Andhra Pradesh | 1. Budgetary allocation by the state government.
2. Grants, donations, and gifts from central, state government/allied authority and private individual and companies
3. Receipts of imposed fines
4. Receipt of compensation recovered from wrongdoer/accused |
|---|---|
| Assam | 1. State government allocates a separate budget for the scheme every year. |
| Bihar | 1. State makes budgetary allocation in the annual budget. Court imposed fines under Sec 357, is also added to the State VCF. CVCF also provides a share through its grant;
2. **District VCF is also constituted in each district which is operated by the Secretary, DLSA upon the sanctions of the Chairman of DLSA.** |
| Chhattisgarh | 1. State Government makes fund provision in budget of Home department |
| Delhi | 1. VC fund from grants-in-aid from the state government, fines, recovered compensation, donations, CSR, operated by SLSA |

Jharkhand	1. State Government shall allot a separate budget for this purpose annually
Madhya Pradesh	1. Victim Compensation Fund will be deposited in Public Account under a new head of account. It shall consist of - 2. State budgetary allocation 3. Receipt of fines imposed 4. Donations and contributions 5. Member secretary of SLSA operates the fund.
Odisha	1. Budget provision by the state 2. Grants, donations, gifts 3. All fines received on or on behalf of the victim's compensation.
Rajasthan	1. State government budget allocation.
Tamil Nadu	1. Operated by the DGP.
Uttar Pradesh	1. VC Fund is operated by the Secretary of SLSA/DLSA.
West Bengal	1. VC Fund is operated by the Secretary of SLSA/DLSA

As shown in the tables above, the DLSA and SLSA have the primary responsibility of recommending and awarding compensation to the victims of human trafficking and other crimes. In terms of functionality, the legal service authorities are expected to investigate cases and accordingly determine the amount of compensation. The legal services authorities are also expected to recommend interim compensation and relief to the victims. However, in most states, there are no independent monitoring and evaluation agencies to evaluate the functioning of VCS. In some states, Andhra Pradesh, Chhattisgarh, and Tamil Nadu, the state home and excise departments have been designated as nodal agencies for monitoring the VCS. Monitoring agencies like the home departments may undertake some evaluation, but in the absence of an independent evaluator, one is forced to think about the effectiveness of the monitoring mechanism given that the home department is also the implementation authority of the scheme.

Functions of Authorities in a Nutshell

Andhra Pradesh	1. Home Department regulates, administers, and monitors the scheme. 2. SLSA is accountable and furnishes regular returns to the Home Department. 3. The state government can also allocate funds to an emergency fund out of the victim compensation fund for interim relief purposes. 4. DLSA decides on the quantum of compensation to be awarded
Assam	1. SLSA responsible for maintaining accounts 2. SLSA places funds at the disposal of DLSA as required
Bihar	1. Member Secretary of SLSA operates the VC fund.
Chhattisgarh	1. Home Department gives allotment to DCs as required 2. DCS maintains account relating to the account and shall return a quarterly report of expenditure to Home Department
Delhi	1. The SLSA can either retain and decide applications for itself or move them to any DLSA for disposal

Jharkhand	1. Operation of the fund by Director, Prosecution, Government of Jharkhand and at the district level operated by District Magistrates 2. DLSA decides the quantum of compensation to be paid to the victim
Madhya Pradesh	1. SLSA is accountable for functions of the scheme and furnishing periodical returns
Odisha	1. VC fund operated by Member Secretary, SLSA) 2. DLSA considers claims and provides financial and support services 3. SLSA makes quarterly returns to the state government
Rajasthan	1. The fund shall be operated by Secretary, SLSA 2. DLSA/SLSA shall examine claims and award compensation
Tamil Nadu	1. DGP will be accountable for his functions and furnish periodical returns of the amounts remitted by the State Government through the Nodal Department
Uttar Pradesh	1. The fund operated by Sec'y of SLSA 2. State government to allot a separate budget for the scheme annually
West Bengal	1. Maintenance of a separate fund namely VC fund with a separate budget allotted for the purpose by the Government, every year. 2. Maintained and audited as per Government rules.

5. Eligibility Criteria for Compensation

Most of the states have laid down common criteria or eligibility for the award of compensation. The basic definition across states is as follows:

Victims must have suffered a loss of injury-causing *'substantial'* loss of income to the family, making it difficult to make ends meet, or have spent substantial money on medical treatment or physical injuries.

There exist serious gaps in this definition, for instance, the word "substantial" is relative and cannot be measured or quantified. The vagueness of terminologies indicates that a victim has to prove the degree of his losses, which is extremely difficult to do. In the absence of which the victim is not entitled to compensation. This problem is particularly serious in cases of human trafficking, including labor trafficking. Is there any scientific technique available to measure the human sufferings of slavery, force, and bondage, or servitude?

Additionally, some of the states have included additional criteria or "terms and conditions" in compensating victims. For instance, in MP, Bihar, Tamil Nadu, and UP schemes have laid down that "victims should not have received compensation concerning the crime from any other scheme of the Central or State Government or insurance company," compensation is subject to the "cooperation of the victim with police and prosecution during the trial," Andhra, Bihar, Jharkhand and Chhattisgarh went a step further and stipulates forty-eight hours for reporting the crime as a condition precedent to grant of compensation. These terms and conditions are proving to be a serious constraint for victims, especially sex and labor trafficking, where due to threat, coercion, etc., they are unable to report the crime or unable to assist the investigation or trial.

Andhra Pradesh	1. The offender is not traced/identified but the victim is identified and where no trial takes place, compensation can be granted. 2. *Victim reports crime within 48 hours of the occurrence of crime.* 3. **The victim cooperates with police from investigation till trial.** 4. The income of the family should not exceed 4.5 lakh per annum.
Assam	1. **The victim/dependant should have reported the crime to the officer-in-charge to Police Station within *48 hours of the occurrence of the crime.*** 2. **Victim/dependant should cooperate with police and prosecution during investigation and trial** 3. When the perpetrator is untraceable/unpunished but the victim is identified and needs to be rehabilitated, compensation can be granted
Bihar	1. Court recommendation or in cases where the offender is inadmissible in court. (untraced/unidentified) 2. **The offender is identified and the trial has already taken place, the victim has cooperated with police and prosecution authority during investigation and trial proceedings.** 3. **The victim/dependant should have reported the crime to the officer-in-charge to Police Station within *48 hours of the occurrence of the crime.***

Chhattisgarh	1. **The victim/dependant should have reported the crime to the officer-in-charge to Police Station within *48 hours of the occurrence of the crime*.** 2. **Victim/dependant should cooperate with police and prosecution during investigation and trial.**
Delhi	1. SLSA/DLSA decides compensation based on the gravity of offense and severity of mental or physical harm or injury, 2. Expenditure incurred on medical treatment for physical and mental health, 3. Impact on employment due to the offense, 4. Whether the abuse was a single incidence or took place over time, the financial condition of the victim, 5. Financial loss to victim and extent/period of same, 6. In case of loss of life, age of deceased, monthly income, number of dependents, life expectancy, future growth prospects.
Jharkhand	1. The offender is not traced/identified but the victim is identified and where no trial takes place, compensation can be granted. 2. ***Victim reports crime within 48 hours of the occurrence of crime.*** 3. **The victim cooperates with police from investigation till trial.**

Madhya Pradesh	1. The recommendation made by the court, DLSA, or SLSA decides the amount of compensation.
2. Compensation to be paid should have occurred within the state. if the crime occurred outside of state and the victim found within the limit of the state, interim relief can be provided
3. Compensation will depend on basis of loss caused to the victim, medical expenses occurred on treatment, minimum sustenance amount required for rehab
Odisha	1. If the victim has not been compensated by any other central or state government scheme.
2. **The victim shall cooperate with police and prosecution from investigation till trial.**
Rajasthan	1. **The victim shall cooperate with police and prosecution from investigation till trial.**
2. The offender is not traced or identified/no trial takes place, and the victim has to incur physical and mental rehab, compensation can be provided
3. **Victim/claimant reports crime without unreasonable delay to Judicial Magistrate**
Tamil Nadu	1. Court recommendation under S. 357A (2) & (3) or when the victim/dependent makes application to SLSA/DLSA.
2. *Victim reports crime within 48 hours of the occurrence of crime.*
3. **Cooperation of the victim with the police and prosecution during investigation and trial.**

Uttar Pradesh	1. *Victim reports crime within 48 hours of the occurrence of crime.* 2. **Cooperation of the victim with the police and prosecution during investigation and trial.** 3. Copy of the order of compensation passed under VCS must be placed on the record of the trial court for the court to pass the order of compensation as per S.357(3) of the Act 4. The implementing authority determines the compensation and rehabilitation services considering the **restorative needs of the victim, LSA has the following parameters:** • Type and severity of the physical injury, medical expenses to be incurred, psychological counseling required by the victim • Age and financial condition of the victim to ascertain his/her educational/professional/vocational training need • Non-pecuniary loss entailing mental suffering, emotional trauma, humiliation.
West Bengal	1. Victim of acid attack and sexual offenses including rape and human trafficking eligible if: • the recommendation is made by the Court, • compensation under 357 is not adequate • the offender is not traced or identified, but the victim is identified, and where no trial takes place

6. Procedure for Grant of Compensation

The procedure in most states is similar, with most states specifying two months as the statutory period:

Where a recommendation is received from the court or an application is made by the victim, the DLSA/SLSA has to examine and verify the facts raised in the claim and after due inquiry, has to decide on the grant of compensation.

A notable exception is Bihar, where the District Criminal Injury Compensation Board examines and the verify the claims of the victim and decides on the quantum of compensation and, condones delays in an application. Based on the board's recommendations the chairman of DLSA passes an order about claim/payment of compensation.

Provision of Interim Relief: All states, except Delhi, have a provision for granting interim relief to the victims of crimes. DLSA/SLSA may order immediate first aid facility or free medical benefits on the certificate of a police officer not below the rank of officer-in-charge or magistrate of the area. Generally, such relief includes medical support and/or first aid facility, as well as any other relief that may be required in the situation, thereby including financial assistance as well.

The period for appeals: In all states where the SLSA is the appellant authority, victims can file an appeal within 90 days of the denial of compensation by DLSA

Adopting NALSA guidelines on a compensation scheme for women victims/survivors of sexual assault/ other crimes – 2018

Andhra Pradesh	No
Assam	No Mention
Bihar	Yes, detailed WVCF
Chhattisgarh	Yes
Delhi	Yes
Jharkhand	Yes
Madhya Pradesh	Yes
Odisha	Yes
Rajasthan	No Mention
Tamil Nadu	Yes, in 2018. Tamil Nadu Victim Compensation Scheme for Women Victims/Survivors of Sexual Assault/other Crimes 2018
Uttar Pradesh	No
West Bengal	Yes, in 2017

7. Quantum of Compensation

The quantum of compensation, provided by the states indicate anomalies. The compensation ranges from as low as Rs. 20,000 in Jharkhand, Rs 10000 in West Bengal, Rs. 100000 in Andhra, Odisha, and Rs. 2,00,000 in Rajasthan and UP, and Rs. 3,00,000 in Assam and Delhi for rehabilitation purposes. In cases of women and child victims of trafficking, the amount varies from Rs. 10000 in Odisha, Rs. 25,000 in Rajasthan, Rs 50,000 in Andhra Pradesh, and Rs 1,00,000 in Tamil Nadu.

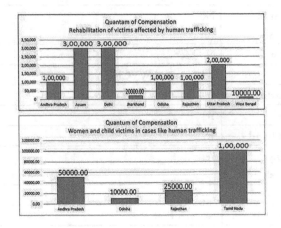

State Wise Performance of VCs

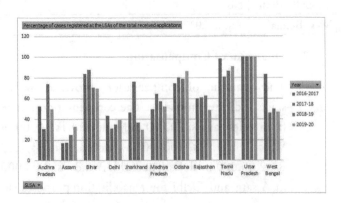

Registration of cases at the Legal Service Authorities

Figure A: Percentage of cases registered with Legal Service Authorities, of total received applications, 2016–2019.

The data analysis of the registered cases at the state and district legal service authorities highlights that only Odisha and Uttar

Pradesh have a higher number of registered cases at LSAs in 2019-20 in comparison to 2016-17. Four states, namely Assam (32.87%), Delhi (39.54%), Jharkhand (29.82%), and Rajasthan (48.65%) have registered cases at LSAs below the 50% mark, showing a greater dependence on court recommendations.

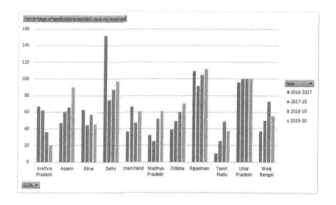

Applications decided vis a vis received

Figure B: State-wise percentage of cases decided vis a vis applied for, 2016-2019

Of the total number of applications received across states, Assam, Madhya Pradesh, Odisha, Rajasthan, and Uttar Pradesh have a greater number of decided cases (vis a vis applications) in 2019–20 than 2016–17. Andhra Pradesh has seen the highest drop in decided cases with only 19.76% of cases being decided in 2019-20, compared to 66.67% in 2016-17. Additionally, data discrepancies could exist with a higher number of decided cases existing in comparison to applications for Delhi (151% in 2016-17) and Rajasthan (108% in 2016-17, 104% in 2018-19, and 111% in 2019-20).

Appendix

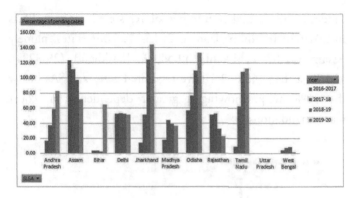

Pendency of applications

Figure C: Percentage of pending applications state-wise, 2016-2019

Across the selected states, only Madhya Pradesh (36.3%), Rajasthan (22.44%), Uttar Pradesh (0%), and West Bengal (1.81%) have pendency of applications below the 50% mark. In certain states, data discrepancies have also been observed, such as a higher number of pending cases than received cases in 2019-20, namely, Jharkhand (143%), Odisha (133%), and Tamil Nadu (112%). Furthermore, Andhra Pradesh (82% in 2019-

20 from 16% in 2016-17) and Bihar (64% in 2019-20 versus 3% in 2016-17) have shown the highest jumps in pendency percentage, compared to other states.

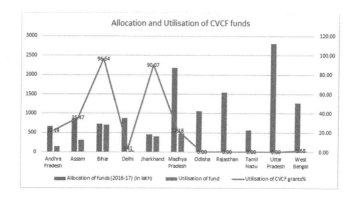

Allocation and Utilization of Central Victim Compensation Fund

Figure D: Allocation and utilisation of Central Victim Compensation funds (2016-17) (in lakhs)

The CVCF is released as a one-time grant to States/UTs to support and supplement their respective victim compensation schemes, with expenditure from this fund only being allowed after the State/UT consumes the non-budgetary resources available to them. Of the selected states, Uttar Pradesh had the highest CVCF allocation in 2016-17 with no utilization. In comparison, Bihar and Jharkhand have the lowest CVCF allocations with 96.5% and 90.07% utilization respectively. This disparity highlights that a better allocation mechanism and rationalisation needs to be prepared at the central level.

1. https://pib.gov.in/Pressreleaseshare.aspx?PRID=1579539